EXPLORE THE SOLAR SYSTEM!

ANITA YASUDA

ILLUSTRATED BY BRYAN STONE

green press INITIATIVE

Nomad Press is committed to preserving ancient forests and natural resources. We elected to print Explore the Solar System! on 30% post consumer recycled paper, processed chlorine free. As a result, for this printing, we have saved:

7 Trees (40' tall and 6-8" diameter)
2,531 Gallons of Wastewater
5 million BTU's of Total Energy
325 Pounds of Solid Waste
610 Pounds of Greenhouse Gases

Nomad Press made this paper choice because our printer, Thomson-Shore, Inc., is a member of Green Press Initiative, a nonprofit program dedicated to supporting authors, publishers, and suppliers in their efforts to reduce their use of fiber obtained from endangered forests.

For more information, visit www.greenpressinitiative.org.

Environmental impact estimates were made using the Environmental Defense Paper Calculator. For more information visit: www.papercalculator.org.

Nomad Press
A division of Nomad Communications
10 9 8 7 6 5 4 3 2 1
Copyright © 2009 by Nomad Press
All rights reserved.
No part of this book may be reproduced in any form without permission in writing from
the publisher, except by a reviewer who may quote brief passages in a review.
The trademark "Nomad Press" and the Nomad Press logo are trademarks of
Nomad Communications, Inc. Printed in the United States.
ISBN: 978-1-9346703-6-1
Illustrations by Bryan Stone
Questions regarding the ordering of this book should be addressed to
Independent Publishers Group
814 N. Franklin St.
Chicago, IL 60610
www.ipgbook.com

Nomad Press
2456 Christian St.
White River Junction, VT 05001

"This logo identifies paper that meets the standards of the Forest Stewardship Council. FSC is widely regarded as the best practice in forest management, ensuring the highest protections for forests and indigenous peoples."

CONTENTS

1 introduction
Let's Explore the Solar System!

3 chapter 1
What Is the Solar System?

14 chapter 2
There's No Place Like Earth

25 chapter 3
Our Star, the Sun

36 chapter 4
Liftoff!

49 chapter 5
Living & Working in Space

61 chapter 6
Meet the Neighbors: the Planets

73 chapter 7
Asteroids, Meteors, & Comets

82 chapter 8
Star Light, Star Bright

Glossary ★ Resources ★ Index

Other titles from Nomad Press in the Explore Your World! Series

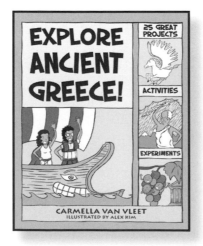

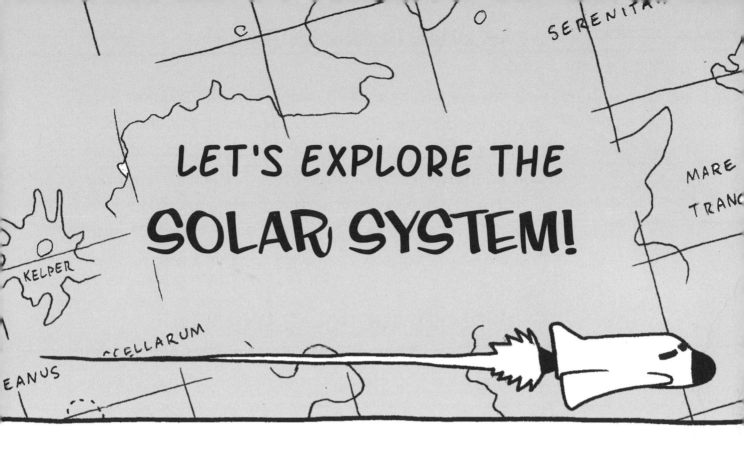

LET'S EXPLORE THE SOLAR SYSTEM!

Have you ever stayed up late at night and looked at the sky? Perhaps you were camping with your family? Once the sun has set it is the moon's turn to shine. The moon's silver light slices across the inky night sky. Maybe you even saw a **satellite**.

☆ ✦ ☆ ★ ☆ ★ ☆ ☆ ✦

Well, people long ago also looked at the same night sky and wondered about it. Were the stars suspended in crystal globes? Was it possible to build a staircase and touch the sky? They did not have high-powered **telescopes** or **probes**. They made up stories about space. They thought they saw chariots and mythical creatures. They imagined it was a place where their dead kings lived.

People all over the world used the stars to find their way. Who knew observing the sky could be a trip into the past? The **solar system** is an amazing place. And our home is here. How did the solar system begin? How large is it? What are the major and minor players in it? You are going to explore the solar system in this book. It's a fantastic place that began billions of years ago! And guess what? Not only is everything around you made of stars, so are you!

GALILEO'S TELESCOPE

EXPLORE THE SOLAR SYSTEM!

This book will answer many of your questions and share some really amazing facts. You'll learn about the planets, astronauts, space shuttles, meteorites, constellations, and ancient observatories. Some of those old observatories are still standing. You'll learn about some interesting people such as Copernicus, Galileo, and Herschel. One of them discovered the center of our solar system. Another was among the first to point a scientific instrument at the sky, and one was the first woman assistant to the court astronomer.

Along the way, we're going to make lots of fun projects, play games, do activities, and hear some silly jokes. Ready? Set? Blast off!

WORDS 2 KNOW

satellite: an object that orbits the earth, or that orbits the sun or another planet.

telescope: a tool used to see objects that are far away.

probe: something used to explore outer space, like a spaceship or a satellite.

solar system: our star system. The collection of eight planets and their moons in orbit around the sun, together with smaller bodies in the form of asteroids, meteoroids, comets, and dwarf planets.

orbit: the path an object makes in space as it circles another object.

WHAT IS THE SOLAR SYSTEM?

Our solar system is only one small star system in the **Milky Way** galaxy. Within a **galaxy** are hundreds of millions, even trillions, of stars and star systems! Scientists estimate there are around 100 billion galaxies in the **universe**.

It's no wonder the universe is so huge that it seems to go on forever. Pretend today is picture day in the Milky Way galaxy. Here they come, the members of the solar system, for their class photo. In the center is the sun, the closest star to us on **planet** Earth. If Earth was the only other member of the solar system it sure would be a small class. But the solar system is anything but small. There are eight planets including Earth.

WORDS 2 KNOW

Milky Way: the galaxy where our solar system is located.

galaxy: a collection of star systems.

universe: everything that exists everywhere.

planet: a large round object in space that orbits the sun.

terrestrial planet: a rocky planet such as Mercury, Venus, Earth, and Mars.

Jovian planet: one of the planets made mostly of gas—Jupiter, Saturn, Uranus, and Neptune.

astronomer: a person who studies the stars, planets, and other bodies in space.

dwarf planet: a small planet in the outer solar system.

moon: a body that orbits a planet.

asteroid: a small, rocky object that orbits the sun.

meteoroid: a rock that orbits the sun. Smaller than an asteroid.

comet: a ball of rocks, ice, and dust that orbits the sun.

gravity: the force that pulls objects toward each other.

CLASS OF 4,600,000,000

Nearest the sun are four small, rocky planets—Mercury, Venus, Earth, and Mars. You can think of these planets as the sun's circle of friends. They are officially called **terrestrial** or inner planets. Standing in the back row are four gas giants or **Jovian** planets—Jupiter, Saturn, Uranus, and Neptune. These planets are much bigger than Earth.

Who is that standing at the classroom door? It's Pluto, an icy world far away from Earth.

JUST FOR LAUGHS

Q What kind of verse does not rhyme?

A The universe.

Astronomers think Pluto is a **dwarf planet.** Sitting in the front row are the smaller members of the solar system, including **moons, asteroids, meteoroids,** and **comets**.

So why are these planets grouped together in the solar system? They all have one very important thing in common. Mercury, Venus, Earth, Mars, Jupiter, Saturn, Uranus, Neptune, and the smaller bodies in space are under the sun's **gravitational** pull. Each planet has an orbit, a path that takes it around the sun. The sun's gravity pulls on the planets and their motions cause them to pull away. It's like a fantastic game of tug of war played out in space.

Now that everyone is here, we can take a picture. "Okay, class—say SOLAR SYSTEM!"

HOW WAS THE SOLAR SYSTEM CREATED?

Today we are going to make a birthday cake for the solar system. We will need many candles: 4.6 billion candles, in fact. This is how old scientists think the solar system is. When the solar system was born humans were not around. This means there was no one to record what happened. No reporters, no cameras, and certainly no one to write the events down. What's a scientist to do? Research and collect information, of course.

HAPPY 4.6 BILLIONTH!

then: Ptolemy (90–168 CE) was a Greek scientist who drew a map of space. He thought the sun and all the planets travelled around the earth.

now: We know that the sun is the center of our solar system and that all the planets orbit around it, not around the earth.

FOCUS ON

Nicolaus Copernicus ⭐

Nicolaus Copernicus (1473–1543) was an astronomer with a very unpopular idea. He wrote a book saying that the sun was the center of the solar system. This model of the solar system is called the heliocentric system. *Helio* means "sun" and *centric* means "center." For 2,000 years people had believed the earth was the center of the universe. This is called the geocentric system. *Geo* means "earth." Copernicus's book was banned in many places because his ideas were considered dangerous. The book was banned for 292 years. A crater on the moon is named for him.

Scientists have pieced together the history of the solar system like a giant jigsaw puzzle. And we don't have all the pieces yet!

When the solar system was born there was a giant cloud of dust and gas called a **nebula**. This wasn't the kind of dust that lies under your bed. No, this dust spun around and around. Eventually the nebula began to collapse as gravity forced the cloud to shrink.

Gravity pulled the dust and gas particles until they clustered together. After a long, long time a star we call

STAR PLAYER

The Little Dipper, also called the Little Bear, is home to Polaris, the North Star. When you face Polaris you are looking north. Slaves escaping from southern states followed the North Star. Polaris was an important star for many cultures. Sailors and travelers used the North Star to find their way.

Polaris

the sun formed. Not all the dust and gas was used up in the sun's creation. The rest continued to whirl and spin. Huge rocks collided with each other. Some joined together to become the planets, moons, asteroids, and comets. More solid, rockier planets stayed closer to the sun. Today these are known as Mercury, Venus, Earth, and Mars. Other planets formed farther away from the sun, near the outer reaches of the solar system. These planets are Jupiter, Saturn, Uranus, and Neptune.

HOW BIG IS THE SOLAR SYSTEM?

If you were getting ready to travel across the solar system, it wouldn't be like a car ride with your family. You couldn't simply plug in to a navigation system. For one thing, when the computer asks for your destination you wouldn't know what to enter. Why not? No one knows how large the solar system is or where it ends. It might end when you can no longer feel the sun's gravity. But we don't know for sure.

OUT OF THIS WORLD

In the fourteenth and fifteenth centuries a terrible disease called the "black death" killed many people. They did not know rats were spreading the disease. People were afraid. They tried to guess why it was happening. Some believed an unlucky position of the planets caused the black death.
WOW!

PLANET poem

One way to remember the planets is with this easy saying: **M**y **v**ery **e**ducated **m**other **j**ust **s**erved **u**s **n**achos. The first letter of each word corresponds to the first letter of each planet beginning with the closest to the sun: Mercury, Venus, Earth, Mars, Jupiter, Saturn, Uranus, and Neptune.

nebula: a giant cloud of gas and dust among the stars.

astronomical unit: a unit of measure used in space. The average distance from the earth to the sun, 93 million miles.

Big Bang: the explosion that many scientists think started the universe.

observatory: a place from which astronomers can observe the planets, stars, and galaxies.

The measurements we use on Earth are miles or kilometers. Using these measurements in space would be like trying to measure the earth with grains of rice. Astronomers measure distance in the solar system using an **astronomical unit** (AU) because it is more convenient. One AU is the average distance between the earth and the sun, which is 93 million miles (150 million kilometers). And just think: the sun is the *closest* star to us. If you drove at 60 miles per hour it would take 176 years to reach the sun! Can you imagine how old you'd be if you tried to go farther? Pluto is 40 AU from the sun. With so much to explore we had better get started.

BIG BANG TAG

No one knows for certain how the universe began. Some scientists believe there was a big explosion. This explosion is known as the Big Bang. It created space and the material that formed stars and galaxies.

1 Set up a universe with clear boundaries that are marked using chalk or pylons. One person is the Big Bang. Everyone else scatters across the playing space.

2 The Big Bang cries out "I am the Big Bang. The universe is about to begin. Won't you join in?"

3 The players run or sneak by as the Big Bang tries to tag them. If caught, they become part of the Big Bang. They join hands with the "it" person and try to capture more players.

4 Once all are caught, join hands and huddle together. On the count of three, yell *Big Bang* and spin across the field to form stars, moons, and planets.

Supplies

large open space
boundary markers
group of people

Observe the Stars Like an Astronomer

Ancient astronomers studied the stars and kept records. To begin planning your own **observatory**, choose a place from which to watch the night sky. What can you see? Write it down. Things to look for: What shape is the moon? Do the stars make a pattern? Can you see more than one? Can you see anything moving?

RACE ACROSS THE GALAXY

In the following game the universe is mixed up. Help find the planets and put the solar system back together. The winning players are the ones who can answer the riddles and find the hidden planets.

1 Draw or print out a picture of each planet in our solar system, as well as other celestial bodies, such as the sun and other stars.

2 Write the clues provided here on slips of paper and lay them out on a table. You can make up your own clues if you prefer.

3 Each planet picture needs to be hidden next to an object that will be identified by one of the clues. Have an adult hide the pictures for you.

4 Once the objects are hidden, make sure the clues are spread out on a table so everyone can see them, and start hunting! The individual or team that solves the riddles and finds the most hidden sun, moons, stars, or planets, wins!

Supplies

| paper | a group of |
| colored markers | players |

Here are some ideas for clues:

- I am the closest star to Earth. Find me next to something you wear to protect your eyes.
  A: Sun

10

SCAVENGER HUNT

- I am very fast. Find me in something you wear on your feet. **A: Mercury**

- I am the hottest planet in the solar system. Find me under something that keeps you warm. **A: Venus**

- Flowers grow in me. You will find me in a garden. **A: Earth**

- My name is on a chocolate bar. Look for me in the kitchen. **A: Mars**

- I am a Greek god. A royal person might wear this on his head. Look in a dress-up box. **A: Jupiter**

- Colors swirl around me. You will find me in a jewelry box. **A: Saturn**

- I roll on my side. Look for me in the garage. **A: Uranus**

- The Greek god of the sea. You will find me in the tub. **A: Neptune**

- A famous Disney character shares my name. Find me near the television. **A: Pluto**

- There are billions of me. Look for me near a lamp. **A: stars**

- I'm not made of cheese. Look for me in the refrigerator. **A: the moon**

Tip

YOU CAN MAKE UP YOUR OWN CLUES. YOU COULD INCLUDE ASTRONOMERS AND ASTRONAUTS AS WELL AS COMETS, ASTEROIDS, METEOROIDS, STARS, AND CONSTELLATIONS.

Space Firsts

Yury Gagarin from Russia became the first man in space in 1961.

MAKE YOUR OWN!

ORIGAMI SOLAR SYSTEM MOBILE

All the members of our solar system travel around the sun. The route they travel is called an orbit. Each planet's orbit is different. Like runners at the Olympics, each has a separate lane. The planets do not switch lanes because the sun's gravity keeps them in their place. If there was no gravity the planets would simply spin off into space like bumper cars. Imagine that!

Supplies

colored lightweight paper	wire hanger thin wire or string

1 Fold a 6-inch (15¼-centimeter) square piece of paper in half, top to bottom. Press down hard to make a good crease. Fold in half again, right to left. Make a firm crease again. Spread the paper out flat.

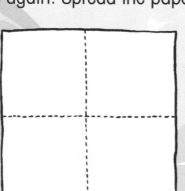

2 Fold opposite corners together to form a triangle. Unfold the paper, then fold the other opposite corners together. Now unfold the paper and spread it flat again. Fold the paper in and down to make a triangle, as shown.

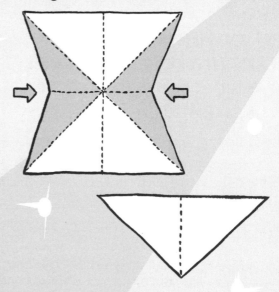

3 Swing the right edge up to left, and down. Swing the right edge up, to the right, and down to form a diamond. Turn over and repeat. Fold the bottom corners to the top point and press down.

5 Use a pencil or your finger to help you. Turn your paper over and repeat step 4. Press down firmly on all the creases one more time.

6 Find the opening in the top. Blow air into the opening to make your origami planet expand into a box. Make seven more.

7 Attach a piece of wire or string to each planet, then tie them to a hanger in order of distance from the sun. You are now ready to hang your mobile.

4 Fold side edges to the center and press down. Turn bottom corners up and crease. Fold and crease again, and tuck the corners into the pockets.

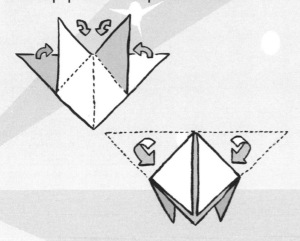

Variation

YOU CAN MAKE DIFFERENT SIZES USING LARGER OR SMALLER SQUARES OF PAPER. DECORATE YOUR PLANETS WITH PAINT, OR GLUE ON SEQUINS, FEATHERS, OR OTHER DECORATIONS. YOU COULD ALSO ADD STAR SHAPES. PAINT OR COVER YOUR HANGER IN YARN. INSTEAD OF ORIGAMI SHAPES, MAKE PLANETS OUT OF TISSUE PAPER STUFFED WITH COTTON BALLS. SECURE THE TOP OF EACH WITH STRING.

THERE IS NO PLACE LIKE EARTH

The third planet from the sun is Earth, our home. It is the largest terrestrial planet. Earth is the only planet whose name isn't from Greek or Roman myths. The word *earth* means ground, or soil. No one knows who named our planet.

☆ ✲ ☆ ★ ☆ ☆ ★ ★ ☆ ☆ ✲

If you could rename Earth, you might want to call it INCREDIBLE. Why? Earth is the only planet we know about that supports life. Many kinds of creatures live here. Scientists don't know how many **species** there are. There could be millions to tens of millions! Many creatures have yet to be discovered. Some of these living things may be very small.

The Southern Cross (the constellation Crux) is the smallest of the constellations. It is best seen from the **Southern Hemisphere**. The Southern Hemisphere is the area of the earth south of the equator. European sailors used the Southern Cross to guide them. Some countries, such as Brazil and Australia, use the image of the Southern Cross on their flags.

Life is present on Earth because of our planet's relationship to the sun. Sunlight takes eight minutes to reach us. Earth's distance from the sun is like a camper being just the right distance from a campfire: not too hot and not too cold. It's just right.

Earth's surface makes it special. It is the only planet with water on its surface. In fact, 71 percent of the earth's surface is covered with water. It has earned us the nickname the Blue Planet. This is our amazing Earth.

THE MOVING EARTH

Did you know you're an astronaut? In fact everyone on Earth is an **astronaut**. So where is our rocket ship? Why, it's right under our feet. Planet Earth of course. Our planet doesn't stand still. It turns at a rate of 1,000 miles an hour. We can't feel it move because Earth spins very smoothly and gravity pulls us onto Earth. But we can see the effects of this movement in the sky.

species: a type of animal or plant.

Southern Hemisphere: the part of the earth that lies south of the equator.

astronaut: a person who travels or works in space.

OUT OF THIS WORLD

The earth zooms around the sun at a speed of 65,000 miles (105,000 kilometers) per hour. Compare this to the fastest jet airplane, which can only reach speeds of 2,000 miles per hour. This means the earth is 32 times faster.

Wow!

When our part of the earth faces the sun, it is day. When it turns away from the sun, it is night.

You may think that the sun is rising every morning, but it is only your place on Earth that has moved. It takes the earth 24 hours—one full day—to make one complete turn.

Earth is also moving in another way. It orbits around the sun. The seasons are not caused by the distance to the sun but by the tilt of the earth. Earth tilts at an angle. The four seasons, winter, spring, summer, and fall, are caused by this tilt. And this tilt changes over the course of a year. So different parts of the globe face

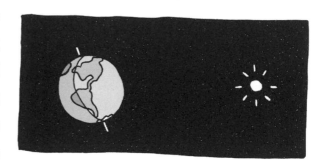

the sun depending on the time of year. When the North Pole tilts toward the sun, it is summer in the **Northern Hemisphere**. When the North Pole tilts away from the sun, it is winter in the Northern Hemisphere. It takes the earth approximately 365 days, or one year, to circle the sun.

EARTH'S ATMOSPHERE

Earth is surrounded by an invisible blanket, the **atmosphere**. The atmosphere is a protective shield that stretches to the edge of space. Other planets have atmospheres

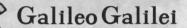

FOCUS ON

Galileo Galilei

Galileo Galilei (1564–1642) made his version of the telescope in 1609. He was one of the first people to use a telescope to study space. His telescope magnified objects 12 times.

Modern telescopes like the Hubble magnify objects a lot more than that! Galileo was the first to see the rings of Saturn and the four moons orbiting Jupiter. Galileo was convinced Earth was not the center of the universe. The leaders of the Roman Catholic Church were so angry with Galileo for teaching this that they had him arrested. He was not allowed to leave his house for the rest of his life.

but none can support life. Ours contains the oxygen we breathe.

Without the atmosphere, people, animals, and plants could not survive. Earth didn't always have so much oxygen. As early life developed oxygen was added to the atmosphere. We have plants to thank for much of the oxygen in our atmosphere. Next time you're talking to your plants, remember to say thank you!

Our atmosphere is fragile. Human activities such as cutting down too many trees and burning **fossil fuels** harm it.

WORDS 2 KNOW

Northern Hemisphere: the part of the earth that lies north of the equator.

atmosphere: the mixture of gases that surround a planet.

fossil fuels: fuel made from the remains of ancient plants and animals.

WORDS 2 KNOW

greenhouse gases: gases that contribute to the warming of Earth's atmosphere.

global warming: an increase in Earth's temperatures.

ozone layer: the layer of the earth's atmosphere that contains ozone and blocks the sun's ultraviolet rays.

crust: the outermost layer of the earth.

mantle: the layer of the earth that lies between the crust and the core.

core: the iron-rich center of the earth.

tectonic plates: moving pieces of the earth"s crust.

Pangaea: a supercontinent that existed on Earth 200 to 300 million years ago.

continent: a large landmass that rises high in the earth's crust.

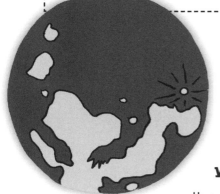

Fossil fuels are natural substances such as coal, oil, and natural gas. When we burn them we release gases called **greenhouse gases** that create pollution. Greenhouse gases cause Earth's temperature to rise. This is called **global warming**. Other gases contribute to the hole in the earth's **ozone layer**. The ozone is a thin layer in the earth's atmosphere that protects us from the sun's harmful rays. Global warming is important to everyone because we share the same atmosphere. We can all help by using less energy.

THEN and NOW FACTOID

then: People long ago had many ideas about Earth's shape. The Egyptians thought the earth was a square. The Babylonians believed Earth was hollow. The Indians imagined a flat Earth resting on huge elephants.

now: Today we know the earth is round, with a bulge in the middle, like a pumpkin. Satellite images show Earth to be 27 miles (43 kilometers) thicker through the middle. Our Earth has a tummy!

LAYERS OF THE EARTH

You might believe Earth is solid when you are jumping and running outside. Solid as a rock. But solid is not the best word to describe Earth. How about moving and changing. Yes, that's right. The earth beneath your feet is alive!

Earth has three main layers. They are the **crust**, the **mantle,** and the **core**. Earth's crust is like your skin, only made of hard rock. The crust is at its thickest under the continents. The crust Is lIke a jigsaw puzzle made of pieces called **tectonic plates**. There are a few dozen major plates. The tectonic plates are constantly moving. This means Earth didn't always look the way it does today.

Once upon a time the tectonic plates were joined together. They formed a giant landmass known as **Pangaea**. Roughly 180 million years ago Pangaea broke up and the pieces slowly moved away from each other. Today on Earth there are six large masses of land called **continents**. The continents are Africa, Antarctica, Australia, Eurasia (Europe and Asia are combined), North America, and South America.

Space Firsts

The first dog in space was Laika, who traveled aboard Sputnik 2 in November 1957.

The continents are still moving today. The tectonic plates float on top of hot, melted rock called the mantle. Where the plates collide, earthquakes, volcanoes, and mountains occur. Beneath the mantle is the core. The outer core contains hot liquid rock. If you could journey to the center of the earth, you would find an iron ball that is 1,500 miles across. That's almost as large as the moon.

THE TELESCOPE

People have always gazed at the sky and wondered what was up there. They tracked the sun, moon, stars, and the visible planets: Mercury, Venus, Mars, Jupiter, and Saturn. They learned to predict the seasons and the phases of the moon. For centuries people believed Earth was the center of the universe. In the 1600s this view would be challenged. In 1608 a Dutch eyeglass maker named Hans Lippershey wrote about his amazing discovery. By looking through two lenses he could make faraway images appear near. The **spyglass** was born!

WORDS 2 KNOW

spyglass: a telescope small enough to hold in your hands.

ellipse: an oval shape.

refracting telescope: a telescope with a lens that gathers light and forms an image of something far away.

convex: a rounded shape like the outside of a bowl.

MAKE YOUR OWN!

ELLIPSE

An ellipse is an oval shape. You will need this ellipse template to make other projects in this book.

1 Place the piece of paper on top of the cardboard. Stick the thumbtacks into the paper a few inches apart. The distance between your thumbtacks will determine how long your ellipse is.

2 Tie one end of the string to one thumbtack. Leaving a little slack in the string, tie the other end to the other thumbtack. The amount of slack you leave in the string will determine the width of your ellipse.

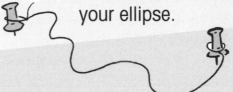

3 Trace the ellipse with the pencil by moving it between the tacks against the string, keeping the string taut. First trace one side of the ellipse, then the other side.

4 Remove the thumbtacks and cut out your ellipse!

TIP YOU CAN USE A RUBBER BAND INSTEAD OF THE STRING. CUT THE RUBBER BAND SO YOU HAVE ONE LONG PIECE OF STRETCHY RUBBER.

Supplies

paper	length of string
cardboard	pencil
thumbtacks	scissors

MAKE YOUR OWN!

PAPIER-MÂCHÉ GLOBE

1 Place your ball or blown-up balloon on a stable base like a bowl so it does not roll.

2 Mix flour with water to form a paste in another bowl. It should be thick enough that it isn't too drippy.

3 Cut or rip pieces of newspaper into long strips. Dip the strips into the paste and place them over your ball or balloon in overlapping layers. Repeat this step many times to make the globe. Let your globe dry.

4 Once the globe is dry ask an adult to cut a slit and pop the balloon. (Skip this step if you used Styrofoam.) Paint the entire globe light blue and let dry.

5 Looking at a map of the world in an atlas or online for help, draw the continents. Paint the continents dark green. Add details with other paint colors. Mark on the globe where you live.

Supplies

Styrofoam ball or balloon	newspaper
2 bowls	scissors
flour	paint brush
water	blue and green paint

MAKE YOUR OWN! MAGNETIC ORBITING EARTH

In the early 1600s a German astronomer named Johannes Kepler studied the orbits of the planets. People believed that all planets orbited in perfect circles. Kepler's research found that every planet's orbit was an ellipse, not a circle.

Tip A GOOD SOURCE FOR MAGNETS IS THE MAGNETIC STRIP ON THE BACK OF A USED CALENDAR.

Supplies

ellipse template	paper
card stock	glue
colored pencils	two magnets

1 Make a large ellipse from your template and trace it onto card stock. Select a point to the left of the center to draw a circle representing the sun. You can color it yellow.

2 Cut out a smaller circle to represent the earth and color it blue. Glue the earth circle to a magnet and place it on the ellipse.

3 Hold the second magnet close enough to the earth to move it along its orbit around the sun. Make sure that you don't hold it so close that the earth jumps off its orbit.

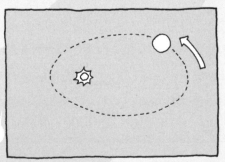

Variation YOU COULD ALSO DRAW THE ORBITS OF OTHER PLANETS.

MAKE YOUR OWN!
MODEL OF A TELESCOPE

Galileo built a refracting telescope. Light enters the far end and passes through a lens. This convex lens bends the light rays until they come into focus. The eyepiece magnifies the light and makes the image appear larger.

1 Cut out two circles of paper for the lenses Galileo used in his telescope. One should be smaller than the other.

2 Place the small circle on a table to act as a base. This circle is the eyepiece.

3 Put modeling clay on the bottom of three straws. Place the straws evenly around the circle.

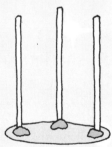

4 Cut one straw into three equal pieces and join with modeling clay to form a triangle.

5 Rest the triangle on the standing straws. This triangle represents the focal point.

6 Repeat the third step and attach three more standing straws to the triangle.

7 Lastly add your second circle. This circle represents the convex lens.

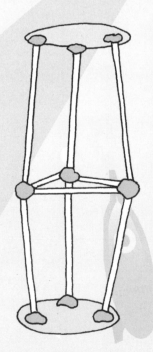

Supplies

| heavy paper | straws |
| scissors | modeling clay |

Variation YOU CAN CHALLENGE YOURSELF BY HAVING YOUR TELESCOPE BALANCE HEAVIER LENSES.

OUR STAR, THE SUN

A blazing light outshines all other objects in the sky. The Greeks called it *helios*. The Romans called it *sol* and the Inca, *Inti*. We call it the sun. It gives Earth light and heat. The sun enables life to grow. What would the earth be without the sun? Our planet would be a lifeless rock in space.

☆ ✹ ☆ ⭐ ☆ ✦ ★ ☆ ☆

Today we know the sun is the closest star to Earth. This is why it looks bigger than all the rest. It's approximately 93 million miles (150 million kilometers) away. The next-closest star is **Proxima Centauri**. It takes light a little more than four years to reach Earth from Proxima Centauri but only eight minutes from the sun.

THE SUN AS KING

People throughout history knew the sun was important. They built observatories to study its movements. Solar observatories were kind of like calendars. They marked important events such as the longest or shortest day of the year. The longest day is called the **summer solstice**. The shortest day is called the **winter solstice**. This information was used to plant and harvest crops.

The sun's ability warmth and light was not understood by early people. They worshipped the sun as a god. In some places you could get into a lot of trouble if you didn't believe the sun was a god. More than 2,500 years ago, a Greek **philosopher** named Anaxagoras said the sun was just a ball of fire. Anaxagoras was kicked out of Athens for this.

Ancient Egyptians believed their king, the pharaoh, was a sun god. King Louis XIV of France called himself the Sun King. Today companies and sports teams use the sun as a symbol of power.

WORDS 2 KNOW

Proxima Centauri: the second-nearest star to Earth.

summer solstice: the longest day of the year. June 21 in the Northern Hemisphere.

winter solstice: the shortest day of the year. December 21 in the Northern Hemisphere.

philosopher: someone who thinks about and questions the way things are in the world.

corona: the outermost part of the sun's atmosphere.

photosphere: the brightest, most visible layer of a star, what we see as the surface. All stars have a photosphere.

solar core: the center of the sun, where it produces its energy.

JUST FOR LAUGHS

Q What kind of sun is cold?

A A sun-dae of course!

Why not associate yourself with the sun? It's the largest object in the solar system, after all. The sun is 300,000 times heavier than Earth. Earth is so small that if the sun were a piñata, one million Earths would fit inside. The sun is king of our solar system.

A GREAT BALL OF GAS

Like most other stars, the sun is a very, very hot ball of gas. It's not solid layers, like the earth, and not liquid, like the oceans. It's made of gas, like air is gas. But in the same way that you can have different kinds of rocks, the sun's gases are very different from our air.

In fact, the sun is made of layers of gas, and each layer has a special name. The outside layer of gas is called the **corona**. The corona looks like a ring of light and is hot, hot, hot. It's 4 million

CORONA

PHOTOSPHERE
CORE

degrees Fahrenheit (2 million degrees Celsius)! Closer to the center of the sun is the **photosphere**. This is the brightest part of the sun. The center of the sun is called the **solar core**. The core Is lIke an extremely hot oven.

OUT OF THIS WORLD

Predicting solar eclipses was a matter of life and death for ancient Chinese astrologers. More than 2,000 years ago, two astrologers said there would be an eclipse. They were wrong, and for this error they lost their heads! Solar eclipses were thought to mean good health and success for an emperor, so the Chinese emperor wasn't too happy when the eclipses didn't happen!

WOW!

It is where the sun can reach temperatures of 27 million degrees Fahrenheit (more than 15 million degrees Celsius). The hottest Earth temperature on record is only 136 degrees Fahrenheit (58 degrees Celsius).

The sun is the only body in our solar system to give out its own visible light. It glows because of **nuclear reactions** in its core. Nuclear reactions create energy. During the nuclear reactions in the sun, the **atoms** of a gas called **hydrogen** bounce around very fast and hit each other. When they

WORDS 2 KNOW

nuclear reaction: when atoms fuse or split apart, releasing a large amount of energy.

atoms: small particles in the universe that make up everything. Atoms are like tiny building blocks, like grains of sand.

hydrogen: a colorless gas that is the most abundant gas in the universe.

fuse: join together.

helium: a colorless gas created in a nuclear reaction in the sun.

hit each other they **fuse** together in a way that turns them into another gas called **helium**. This process creates heat and makes the sun glow. Most of the energy produced in the core passes through the layers of

Space Firsts

Icarus was one of the first mythical travelers into space. Icarus and his father were prisoners on a remote island near Greece. After watching the island's birds, Icarus's father made wings out of wax and feathers so they could fly away and escape. He warned his son not to fly too close to the sun or else the wax on the wings would melt. Icarus did not listen to his father. He flew so close to the sun that his wings melted, and he fell into the sea.

the sun until it reaches the photosphere. Then it spreads into space as heat and light. Earth receives a small portion of the sun's energy.

SPOTS, FLARES, AND PROMINENCES

The sun is always spinning, just like the earth. This is called **rotation**. But the sun's rotation is not smooth because the sun is not solid. Many amazing effects, such as **sunspots**, are created by the sun's uneven rotation. Sunspots are storms on the sun. Galileo saw sunspots through 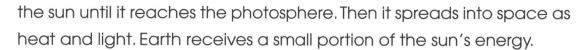 his telescope but he couldn't explain them. Sunspots appear as dark patches on the surface of the sun. They are not as hot as the rest of the sun's surface. Most are many times bigger than Earth. They can last for hours or months. Larger explosions of gas into space are called **solar flares**. Gas can also form huge loops called **prominences**.

Sunspots, flares, and prominences affect us on Earth. Studies show that fewer sunspots lead to cooler temperatures on Earth. **Particles** in solar flares can disrupt radios and cell phones on Earth. They can even damage satellites. Solar flares cause **auroras** here on Earth.

WORDS 2 KNOW

rotation: turning all the way around.

sunspot: a dark area on the sun's surface that is cooler than the surrounding area.

solar flare: a sudden burst of energy from the sun's surface.

prominence: something that sticks out. On the sun it's a stream or loop of gas.

particle: tiny piece of something.

aurora: visible colored light in the night sky around the North and South Poles.

FOCUS ON

Isaac Newton

As a child, Sir Isaac Newton (1642–1727) kept a journal of observations. He liked to record what he saw around him! Later, when Isaac grew up he studied math and astronomy at school. He showed how **gravity** applied to everything in the universe. Sir Isaac Newton used this information to predict the movement of stars as well as of the planets around the sun. He also constructed the first **reflecting** telescope. A reflecting telescope uses a curved mirror instead of a lens to collect light.

AURORAS

Auroras are colored, swirling lights. They dance in the night sky in Earth's far north and south. In the north these beautiful lights are called the **aurora borealis**, or Northern Lights. In the south they are called the **aurora australis**, or Southern Lights. Sometimes we can see the Northern Lights as far south as all over the United States.

Since ancient times people have watched and respected the auroras. The Inuit in Canada's north believed the lights were the souls of animals dancing. The Maoris of New Zealand thought the glowing sky was caused by campfires started by their ancestors.

THEN AND NOW FACTOID

then: The ancient Chinese believed an eclipse took place when a dragon was eating the sun. They banged on drums, pots, and anything else that could produce a loud sound. They thought this loud noise would scare off the dragon and let the sun return.

now: We know that a **solar eclipse** is caused when the moon blocks the light from the sun. A **lunar eclipse** is when the earth passes between the sun and the moon, casting a shadow.

WORDS 2 KNOW

gravity: the force that pulls objects toward each other. It holds you to the earth's surface.

reflecting telescope: a telescope that uses a curved mirror to collect light.

aurora borealis: colored lights seen in the sky around the North Pole.

aurora australis: colored lights seen in the sky around the South Pole.

solar eclipse: when the moon moves between the sun and the earth, blocking the sun's light.

lunar eclipse: when the earth passes between the sun and the moon, casting a shadow on the moon.

solar wind: the flow of many tons of tiny particles from the sun's surface into space each second.

In medieval Europe people thought the auroras were magical. When they saw the auroras they believed something bad was about to happen.

Scientists now know the auroras are caused by the **solar wind**. The solar wind is a stream of gas released from the sun. Solar winds give off tons of tiny particles. Some particles in the solar wind collide with gases in the earth's atmosphere. Each gas glows in a different color so auroras appear in many colors. Auroras can be green and yellow. Red can mix in. Sometimes there is purple and blue, too. Be a sky watcher and you may catch a glimpse of these sparkling lights.

MAKE YOUR OWN!

ANCIENT SOLAR OBSERVATORY

Ancient peoples tracked the seasons by looking at the location of the rising or setting sun. Predicting the seasons was important to know when to plant crops. You're going to make a model of a solar observatory based on one at the Cahokia Mounds site in Illinois that people today call Woodhenge. It's a series of wooden posts used as a calendar. The posts line up with the rising sun at certain times of the year. This cooking activity uses a stove, so ask an adult to help. Be sure to wash your hands.

1 Follow the directions on the cereal box to make Rice Krispies Treats. Ask an adult to help you as you'll need to use the stove. Let the mixture cool for a few minutes.

2 Line a metal baking sheet with wax paper. Spread the cereal mixture out evenly.

3 Place the baking sheet in the fridge and let it cool. Note that if you let the Rice Krispies Treats cool completely they will be difficult to cut. Use your ruler and cut the Rice Krispies Treats into even blocks to represent the wooden posts of Cahokia's sun circle.

Hint SMEAR A LITTLE BUTTER ON THE BASE OF EACH BLOCK TO HELP THEM STAND.

Supplies

stove	baking sheet
Rice Krispies cereal	wax paper
margarine or butter	refrigerator
bag of marshmallows	knife
large saucepan	ruler
wooden spoon	tray

4 Place the blocks upright in a circle on a tray. Now, you're ready to serve your friends a tasty version of a Cahokia solar observatory.

MAKE YOUR OWN!

SOLAR OVEN

You don't need a campfire to cook outside. You can also cook with the sun's energy. It's that strong! Temperatures in your solar oven can reach 275 degrees Fahrenheit, so be certain to do this activity with an adult present.

1 Cover the inside of a pizza box, including the lid, with foil. Place a small cooking tin in the center.

2 Assemble s'mores by placing chocolate and a marshmallow between two graham crackers. Place the s'mores in the baking tin.

3 Cover the tin with the plastic bag to keep the heat in. Place the solar oven in the sun. You'll know your s'mores are ready when the chocolate is melted.

Supplies

pizza box	chocolate
tin foil	marshmallows
baking tin	clear plastic bag
graham crackers	oven mitt

4 The oven can reach high temperatures. Ask an adult to use an oven mitt to remove the tin and peel off the plastic. Now that your s'mores are done, share them with your fellow space explorers.

Variation

YOU CAN USE A SHOEBOX OR ANY OTHER SIMILAR SIZED BOX WITH A LID. YOU DON'T HAVE TO STOP WITH S'MORES. HOW ABOUT FLATBREAD PIZZA OR QUESADILLAS?

MAKE YOUR OWN! SOLAR ECLIPSE

Long ago eclipses were not understood. It was frightening to see daylight disappear as a black disc slowly slid in front of the sun. It was as if the sun had left Earth for good. The word *eclipse* comes from a Greek word meaning "abandon" or "leave." Follow the instructions below to see how an eclipse really works. Remember to never look directly at the real sun as that may damage your eyes.

Supplies

- small box (rectangular)
- scissors
- construction paper, black & other colors
- yellow tissue paper
- glue and tape
- toothpick
- markers

1 Cut out a window at both ends of your box. Make a slit across the top of the box, midway between the ends.

2 From construction paper, cut out a square small enough to fit through the slit.

3 In the center of this small square, draw a circle and cut it out. Glue a piece of yellow tissue paper over the hole to create a mini stained glass window. Set to one side.

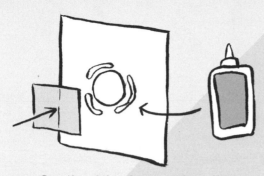

4 On the black construction paper, draw a circle smaller than your first one to represent the moon. Cut the circle out and glue or tape it to a toothpick.

5 Draw two dragons on either side of the box to represent the Chinese solar eclipse myth. Decorate your box with brightly colored paper.

6 Insert the yellow slide, and hold your box toward the light to see your sun shine.

7 To create an eclipse insert the moon in front of the yellow slide and hold it to the light. You can move the moon slowly across the sun to show how an eclipse looks from when the moon just starts to cover the sun to when it covers it completely.

ST★R PLAYER

Cygnus, or the Swan, is also called the Northern Cross. Not all cultures throughout history have seen this constellation as a swan. It has been called a horned owl, an ibis, an eagle, and a hen. An ibis is a bird from ancient Egypt. One Greek myth tells of Orpheus the musician. When he played his lyre, a stringed instrument, all the animals came to listen. After he died he was placed in the heavens as a swan near the stars of his lyre.

LIFTOFF!

That bright shining circle in the night sky is the moon. Humans have put thousands of satellites into space. But we didn't launch the moon. It's Earth's only natural **satellite**. It revolves around Earth as our planet orbits the sun. Wherever Earth goes, the moon follows.

☆ ⁎ ☆ ⭐☆ ⁎ ⭐ ☆ ☆⁑

Other planets have moons, too. Some planets have dozens and dozens of moons. But the moon is special to us because we only have one and it's our own. And human beings have been there. Astronauts have bounded along the surface, driven moon buggies there, collected rock samples, planted a flag, and even played golf on it!

Robert Goddard

When Robert Goddard (1882–1945) was 17 years old, he climbed up a cherry tree in his backyard. There, he dreamed of traveling to Mars. Years of study and hard work led Robert to believe space flight was possible. He was the first to launch a liquid fuel rocket. At the time of his death he held 214 **patents** in rocketry. He is now called the "father of modern rocketry."

Scientists have studied the moon for years. But there are still many mysteries. No one is certain how the moon formed. Of course there are several ideas. One popular idea is that billions of years ago, an object the size of a small planet crashed into Earth. The force of this crash melted Earth's crust. Hot rock blasted into space like fireworks. Over a long time some of this material joined together to become the moon.

Though the moon may have had its origins on Earth, it is very different from our planet. The moon has less gravity than Earth. This is a result of its size.

JUST FOR LAUGHS

Q What do you get if you cross the moon with a flashlight?

A A moonbeam.

🚀 **satellite:** an object in space that orbits a larger one.

patent: when an invention is protected from being illegally copied.

The moon is only one-quarter the size of Earth. With less gravity to pull you down, you can jump higher and stand taller on the moon. But you need a space suit because there is no atmosphere. That means no air to breathe.

There is also no weather. Think about a place with no wind or rain. A weather forecaster's job on the moon would be dull. "Good morning, residents of the moon," the forecaster would say. "You can expect another dry, dusty day. More drastic temperatures are in store. In the sun it will be a hot 225 degrees Fahrenheit (107 degrees Celsius). At the poles it will be in the minuses. Tonight, temperatures will plummet to minus 300 degrees Fahrenheit (minus 184 degrees Celsius). Tomorrow your forecast will be the same." This doesn't mean everything stays the same all the time. A forecaster might have to interrupt his broadcast for this common occurrence—a **meteorite** strike. There's no atmosphere to protect the moon's surface, so it's constantly hit by meteorites.

Take a Walk on the Far Side

Only one side of the moon faces Earth and is visible to us. The invisible side is called the **far side**. In 1959 a Russian spaceship called Luna 3 was the first to fly past the far side. The photographs were amazing. They showed a heavily cratered moon.

THEN AND NOW FACTOID

then: Ancient civilizations believed changes in the moon were magical.

now: We know that the phases of the moon are caused by the angle of the sun's light.

THE MOON'S SURFACE

From Earth we only see one side of the moon. This side has dark and light regions. The Japanese imagined the dark patches to be a rabbit making rice cakes. Europeans saw a man's face. Galileo looking through his telescope thought they were filled with water. People gave the dark spots romantic names like the Ocean of Storms and the Sea of Showers. In Latin, the language of the ancient Romans, they were called **maria**, meaning "seas."

There are, in fact, no men, bunnies, or seas on the moon. Instead, a thick layer of dust covers the surface. The maria do not contain water. They are just low areas with fewer **craters**. Scientists believe they are the result of lava that once flowed from volcanos on the moon. One, called the Sea of Tranquility, was the site of the first lunar landing.

WORDS 2 KNOW

far side of the moon: the side of the moon that faces away from Earth.

meteorite: a piece of a meteoroid that has landed on a planet or moon.

maria: lowland seas.

crater: large bowl-shaped hole in the ground caused by an asteroid's impact.

The light patches on the moon are hilly areas covered with craters. Some craters are several inches wide and others are up to 700 miles (1,126 kilometers) across. Craters on the moon have formed over billions of years from the impact of meteorites hitting the moon.

OUT OF THIS WORLD

What has over two and a half million parts? Only the most intricate machine ever made—the space shuttle.
WOW!

MOON PHASES

During the course of a month the moon appears to change shape. The moon's different shapes are called **phases**. As the moon circles Earth we only see the part of the moon that reflects the sun's light. How much of the moon we can see depends on the position of the moon in its orbit. The bright side faces toward the sun. The part in darkness faces away from the sun.

Ancient people thought the moon's changes were magical. The Inuit of Greenland believed the moon god

WORDS 2 KNOW

phases: the changing appearance of the moon during a month.

lunar cycle: the phases that the moon goes through, from crescent moon to full moon and back again.

crescent moon: when less than half of the moon is showing.

full moon: when the whole moon shows.

lunar month: the period between the beginning and end of the moon's cycle.

Space Firsts

Astronaut Alan Shepard was America's first man in space, in 1961. When he was a boy he would help push the planes in and out of a local airport hangar. When he grew up he flew planes, and in 1971 Alan commanded the Apollo 14 mission to the moon.

chased his sister, the sun, each month, in a never-ending game of tag. The moon enjoyed the chase so much he forgot to eat. He became very skinny until he remembered to eat again. This describes the **lunar cycle**.

It takes the moon an average of 29½ days to go from a **crescent moon** to a **full moon** and back again. Our calendar is based on this lunar cycle. The word *month* actually comes from the word *moon*.

In Latin, the word for "moon" is *luna*. This is where the words *lunar* and *lunatic* come from. The full moon has always been linked to odd happenings. The phases of the moon were often wrongly linked to strange behavior in people and animals. There are stories from around the world of people being turned into werewolves at the sight of a full moon. In Greek mythology, King Lycaon was changed into a wolf for playing a trick on Zeus, the Greek god of the sky.

A Moon Made of Cake

The moon festival is celebrated on the 15th day of the eighth **lunar month** in many Asian countries and communities. A family might prepare special food, tell traditional stories, and sing songs, all by the light of the moon. A popular sweet is a moon cake. Moon cakes are made of red bean or lotus paste. They are wrapped in pastry and topped with a duck egg to represent the moon.

Space Race Capsule

In 1957 the Soviet Union launched Sputnik 1, the first artificial satellite. This began the race to the moon. **NASA** also launched a series of probes. In 1961, the Russian astronaut Yury Gagarin became the first human in space. Finally, in 1969, an American named Neil Armstrong became the first person to step foot on the moon.

FLY ME TO THE MOON

The dream of space exploration and landing on the moon excited many scientists. It wasn't easy getting people to the moon. Animals were used as astronauts at first. The United States and the **Soviet Union** put a lot of effort into safely landing a man on the moon. This was called the **space race**.

America's Apollo 11 was the first spacecraft with people on board to land on the moon. Neil Armstrong and Edwin "Buzz" Aldrin were those first people to explore the moon. On July 20, 1969, Neil Armstrong declared, "That's one small step for man, one giant leap for mankind." The two astronauts spent a total of 21 hours on the moon. They took photographs and collected rock and soil samples. Ten more astronauts traveled to the moon in the Apollo program between 1969 and 1972.

The first space shuttle, named Columbia, was launched in 1981. Since then close to 500 people have been into space! But no one has set foot on the moon since the Apollo project. Maybe the next person could be you!

Soviet Union: a former country that included present-day Russia.

space race: the race between countries to successfully land an astronaut on the moon.

NASA: stands for the National Aeronautics and Space Administration. The U.S. organization that is in charge of space exploration.

MAKE YOUR OWN!

EDIBLE PHASES OF THE MOON

When the moon travels around the earth it appears to change shape. These shapes are called phases. There are eight phases of the moon. Here we are going to recreate four. The phases you will make are the new moon, crescent moon, half moon, and full moon.

1 Cut two mini bagels in half. Do not put any cream cheese on the first half of bagel number one. Set it aside. This is the new moon, which is completely or almost dark.

2 On the second half of that bagel, smear a small sliver of cream cheese on the right side. This is the crescent moon.

3 On bagel two, smear cream cheese on the right side of one of the halves, to create a half-moon.

4 On the fourth bagel half, smear cream cheese all over the bagel to create a full moon. A full moon is when the lit side of the moon faces toward Earth. Invite your family or friends to share your phases of the moon snack.

Variation YOU CAN ALSO USE CHOCOLATE COOKIES AND ICING SUGAR FOR THIS PROJECT.

MAKE YOUR OWN!

SPACE SHUTTLE

The first Space Shuttle blasted off on April 12, 1981. Before the Space Shuttle, spacecraft were not reusable. They were only used for one space voyage. Some parts were left in space and others burned up in the atmosphere. So how did astronauts return to Earth safely? They returned in special capsules that broke off from the spacecraft. These capsules had parachutes and they landed in the ocean.

1 Rinse out a lemonade carton and let dry. Wrap the carton with felt or fabric and cut to size. Glue the material to the carton.

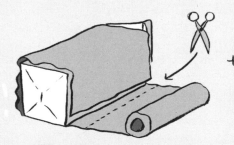

2 Cut out a felt circle with a diameter equivalent to the length of the carton. The circle should be as wide as the carton's length.

3 Fold the circle in quarters and cut along one quarter to the center. Overlap and glue the circle edges to form a cone shape.

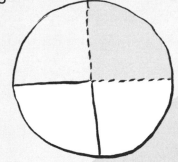

Supplies

fresh or frozen lemonade carton

scissors

pieces of felt, or fabric scraps such as a flannel shirt, blanket, etc.

white glue

cardboard

4 Glue this piece to the top of the carton to form the nose of the shuttle. From a contrasting piece of fabric, cut out the wings and glue these in place. You can glue pieces of cardboard to the fabric to help the wings hold their shape.

5 From a third piece of fabric, cut out the rocket's flames and glue them to the bottom edge of the shuttle.

6 Cut out a small circle from green or blue fabric to represent Earth and place this near the top of the craft. Your astronauts now have a view of home.

STAR PLAYER

Canis Major, or the Big Dog, is one of Orion's two hunting dogs. Orion was the Greek god of hunting. The Canis Major constellation contains Sirius, the brightest star in the night sky. Have you heard the expression the "Dog days of summer"? This expression comes from the fact that Sirius, called the Dog Star, appears in the Northern Hemisphere in late July and August. People 2,000 years ago thought that Sirius's added heat caused the hot days of summer.

MAKE YOUR OWN!

RACE TO THE

With inventions such as space probes, rockets, and satellites, the dream of landing on the moon became a reality. It wasn't without many difficulties, though. Try your luck at landing on the moon.

Supplies

paper	markers
scissors	2 to 3 players
pencil	tokens
poster board	dice
glue	

1 Cut out 20 squares of paper. Write one of the following phrases on each square:

- Blast Off!
- You are a successful test pilot, move ahead four spaces.
- Accepted into astronaut training, move ahead two spaces.
- Swim 25 meters in a pool with your flight suit on. Roll again.
- Sleep late and miss class, move back to start.
- Selected for the mission, move ahead one space.
- G-A chimp is selected, move back one space.
- Rocket doesn't work, miss a turn.
- Help redesign the rocket, move ahead one space.
- Rocket breaks through Earth's gravitational pull, roll again.
- Help to navigate the rocket. Move ahead two spaces.
- Spacecraft misses the moon, move back to start.
- You are interviewed from space, miss a turn.
- Help with an onboard experiment, move ahead three spaces.
- Your sandwich makes crumbs in the cabin, move back three spaces.
- Successfully check all systems, move ahead one space.
- Your rocket orbits the moon, take another turn.
- Board a small landing craft, roll again.
- You forget to bring the flag, move back three spaces.
- You have landed!

MOON BOARD GAME

2 After you have written on all of the squares, arrange them in a pattern on the poster board. Glue them down. Then decorate your game board with the markers. You can draw spaceships and rockets as well as stars, planets, and moons.

TO PLAY

1 Each player places a token on the first square, Blast Off. To decide who goes first, players take turns rolling one of the dice. The high roller is the player to go first in the game.

2 Player #1 rolls one of the dice and moves the correct number of spaces. Once there, he or she follows the instructions to move forward or back, lose a turn, or roll again.

3 Then, he or she waits for his or her next turn. If there are no instructions to move, the player remains on the square until his or her next turn.

4 Players take turns rolling, moving, and following instructions. To win, a player must roll the exact number needed to land directly on the last square.

GYROSCOPE

Gyroscopes are amazing and fun. When you spin a gyroscope, its axle keeps pointing in the same direction. A gyroscope helps keep a spacecraft on course. Gyroscopes are used on airplanes, space stations, shuttles, and even the Hubble space telescope.

Supplies

- cardboard box
- scissors
- tape
- toothpicks
- hollow plastic drink sticks
- modeling clay

1 Cut out two discs from the cardboard box. Label them A and B. Disc B should be able to move freely within disc A.

2 Cut out a small circle to fit in the center of disc B. Label it C. Cut two stir sticks so their lengths equal the widths of disc A and disc B.

3 Tape stir sticks to discs A and B. Insert a toothpick to join the stir sticks. Be sure to tape the ends so the toothpick doesn't fall out.

4 Repeat step 3, this time taping the stir sticks on the opposite sides of disc A and B.

5 Tape a stir stick down the middle of circle C, making sure it extends beyond the circle's edges.

6 Cut two stir stick pieces to match the width of disc B. Tape them to disc B, making sure they line up with stir sticks attached to circle C. See image.

7 Insert toothpicks into the stir sticks to join disc B to circle C.

8 Tape a stir stick to disc A at the axis. Place this last stick into a modeling clay base. Now you can spin your gyroscope.

LIVING & WORKING IN SPACE

Have you ever woken up in the morning, and just rolled over and gone back to sleep? Well "Good Morning" takes on a whole new meaning in space. Astronauts experience 16 sunsets every 24 hours! This means a new day begins nearly every 90 minutes!

☆ ✶ ☆ ⭐︎☆ ✶ ✶ ☆ ☆ ✷

Astronauts still stick to a 24-hour daily routine because that's what humans are used to. Each day is carefully planned by **mission control**, with 8.5 hours set aside to rest. Gazing out the window must be fun, but astronauts also have real work to do. They have to install equipment or do science experiments. Astronauts are responsible for cleaning the spacecraft and making their own meals. These are only a few of their inside jobs. There's even more to do outside.

Space walks are exciting. Astronauts must leave the comfort of a spacecraft for the darkness of space. In space it's difficult for an astronaut to move around. There is no land, air, or water to push against. Astronauts need strong arms to propel themselves, as a space walk usually lasts five to seven hours. How thrilling it would be to ride on the end of the robotic arm as you free fall toward Earth! This is all part of the day's work of an astronaut.

WORDS 2 KNOW

mission control: a command center on Earth that helps astronauts complete their mission.

microgravity: when gravity is very low.

weightless: the sensation of having no gravity pulling you down.

WEIGHTLESSNESS

Living and working in space presents challenges. There is gravity in space, but it's low. The moon also has low gravity. An environment with low gravity is called **microgravity**. When there is zero gravity, astronauts are **weightless**. This doesn't mean astronauts weigh less. They just can't feel their own weight. You can only feel weight if something pushes against you. Astronauts float in the microgravity of space because the movement of the orbiting spaceship balances the gravity to make them weightless.

So why doesn't a spaceship crash into Earth? Spacecraft travel very fast as they orbit Earth. They travel so fast, in fact, that gravity pulls them in a circle around Earth.

JUST FOR LAUGHS

Q What do you call an astronaut who eats peanut butter in space?

A An astro-nut.

Floating in space may seem cool to you, but some astronauts complain that it makes them sick. On Earth our body knows what is up or down. In space there is no up or down. Without gravity to push against, bones and muscles become weak. Because of that, it's important for astronauts to be fit. To stay fit in space, astronauts have to exercise each day. This also allows them to recover more easily from the effects of space travel when they return to Earth.

INTERNATIONAL SPACE STATION

Where do astronauts live in space? On a space station, of course. The first space station was the Salyut 1. It was launched in 1971 by the Soviet Union. Technology has come a long way since then. Since 2000, astronauts from over 16 countries have lived and worked on the new International Space Station. The station is like a giant floating science experiment. Every day is a challenge for the astronauts. They have to learn to work together and work well with machines in space. Information gathered from the International Space Station may be used for future journeys into deep space. Maybe a journey that will be undertaken by you!

INTERNATIONAL SPACE STATION FACTS

• The International Space Station has over 100 major components.

• Once completed, the new space station will be bigger than a football field (360 feet long and 290 feet across or 110 meters long and 88 meters across). This will make it the biggest structure ever built in space.

• The International Space Station travels at 17,500 miles (28,163 kilometers) per hour.

• It will take 46 separate space missions and 166 space walks to assemble the new space station.

• The entire station is powered by solar panels that cover almost an acre (0.4 hectare).

• The International Space Station orbits Earth 16 times a day.

• The International Space Station is one of the brightest objects in the night sky.

• Every six months it is necessary to send supplies of oxygen, food, and water to the International Space Station.

It's possible to see the International Space Station from almost anywhere on Earth. A website called Heavens Above www.heavens-above.com tells you when the International Space Station will be visible from your hometown. Under configuration, click "select from map" to set your location and choose your time zone. Then under satellite you can select a 10-day prediction for ISS, the International Space Station.

THEN AND NOW FACTOID

then: Space suits used in the Apollo mission, including the life-support backpack, weighed about 180 pounds (81 kilograms). They were designed to be lightweight to allow astronauts to work on the moon.

now: Shuttle suits weigh around 280 pounds (127 kilograms) including life-support systems. They are designed to be worn only in microgravity.

FOCUS ON

Neil Armstrong

Neil Armstrong (1930–) started taking flying lessons when he was just a teenager. He received his pilot's license before he could even drive a car! When he grew up, Neil worked as a naval aviator and test pilot before becoming an astronaut. He commanded Apollo 11, and he was the first person to step on the moon's surface. Neil Armstrong and fellow astronaut Edwin "Buzz" Aldrin explored the moon's surface for two and a half hours.

SPACE CLOTHING

Clothing worn in a spacecraft looks a lot like something you might wear on Earth. Astronauts put on pants or shorts and T-shirts to exercise in, just like you. But their clothing has a lot more Velcro and pockets. This is so things don't float away.

What an astronaut wears outside a spacecraft is quite special. Space suits are amazing. One size fits all, and each suit weighs a staggering 280 pounds (127 kilograms) on Earth. One suit costs roughly 12 million dollars! Space suits protect astronauts from the hot sun. They also provide an atmosphere the astronaut can breathe in. They're equipped with communication devices, water pouches with a drinking straw, and even a urine collector! That's right, there are no bathroom breaks allowed on a space walk.

SPACE FOOD

Space travel is like camping. Don't leave anything important behind. Astronauts can't run to the local corner store for supplies. And restaurants don't deliver to space. At least they don't deliver yet. Months before blasting off into space, missions are carefully planned out. And this means food, too. Astronauts eat three meals a day plus snacks.

In early space flights, food was often in liquid form. Astronauts had to squeeze their food out of toothpaste-like tubes. Or they had to try to swallow gelatin-coated food cubes. But now there are many types of food to choose from. The menu on a spaceflight may rival your local family restaurant. In 2007, China launched its first astronauts into space. They had 20 different foods to choose from, including spicy and sour shredded meat and rice.

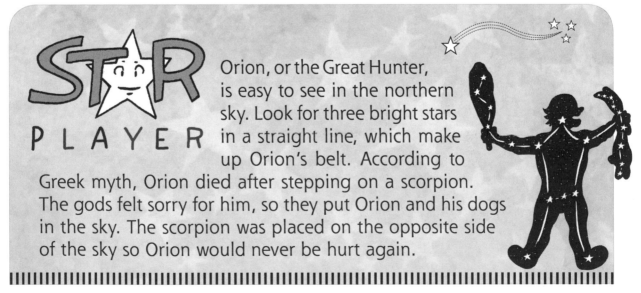

STAR PLAYER

Orion, or the Great Hunter, is easy to see in the northern sky. Look for three bright stars in a straight line, which make up Orion's belt. According to Greek myth, Orion died after stepping on a scorpion. The gods felt sorry for him, so they put Orion and his dogs in the sky. The scorpion was placed on the opposite side of the sky so Orion would never be hurt again.

With no refrigerator on board, food has to stay fresh for the entire mission without being kept cold. Food is prepared so astronauts can eat one bite at a time. They're careful not to make crumbs. Crumbs float in space. They could end up in an astronaut's eyes or the air vent. Some foods have to be prepared by adding water. Once their meal is ready, astronauts use food trays equipped with straps to hold plates down and scissors to cut open food packages. Now they're ready to tuck in.

Water

In space, water doesn't behave as it does on Earth. It doesn't run down your body, it clings to you! Instead of a hot bath or shower, astronauts on the Space Shuttle use a special soapy cloth to keep clean. The International Space Station has a freshwater hose for astronauts to use. Instead of rinsing off, a separate vacuum hose sucks away the dirty water.

SPACE SLEEP

Sleep is just as important in space as it is on Earth. Astronauts need to be well rested in order to perform the next day. Often it's hard for

them to fall asleep. There are the sounds of machines humming and fellow astronauts moving about to cope with. And one of them might snore! But the biggest obstacle to falling asleep is weightlessness.

In microgravity astronauts can sleep anywhere. Some astronauts sleep in their pilot seats. Others fasten themselves to a wall, seat, or bunk so they don't float around. There's no up or down in space so an astronaut may be sleeping vertically or horizontally in a sleeping bag. To make bunks a little more Earth-like, they come equipped with a pillow, a light, and even a blanket to help keep the noise out.

OUT OF THIS WORLD

Can you grow in space? Yes, it's true. The lack of gravity means that astronauts grow several inches or centimeters during a space mission. With no gravity to push down on them, an astronaut's spine stretches. They won't remain this height, though. Back on Earth their height returns to normal.

WOW!

Before they can say sweet dreams, astronauts cross their arms. If they don't, their arms will float above their heads.

In the morning, NASA plays a short recording to rouse astronauts from sleep. This is called a wake-up call. A lively song sets the mood for the day. It also reminds the crew that there is an entire team back on Earth cheering them on. Visit the NASA web site to learn about astronauts and their days in space.

Space Firsts

On June 3, 1965, Edward Higgins White made history when he exited the hatch of Gemini 4 to become the first American to perform a space walk. His suit and special hand-held propulsion unit were not even certified for use in space until 10 days before the launch! When the hand unit ran out of fuel, Ed was forced to use a 25-foot tether to maneuver himself.

SPACE FIRSTS

MAKE YOUR OWN! 'ROBOTIC' ARM

The Canadarm 2 is a robotic arm designed to move end-over-end to reach many parts of the space station. It was invented in Canada and that's how it got it's name! The Canadarm has seven motorized joints. Sensors provide it with a sense of touch. In orbit, the arm is able to maneuver a space shuttle.

1 Cut out four pieces of cardboard, each 12 by 2 inches (30 by 5 centimeters). Poke a small hole in the center of each piece.

2 Join two pieces together to form a cross by pushing a brad through and bending back the ends to secure. Repeat with the other two pieces.

3 Poke a hole an inch in from two of the ends on one of the crosses. Poke a hole an inch in from all ends on the other cross.

4 Join the crosses by centering the holes and pushing a brad through. Bend back all the ends.

5 Cut out two more pieces of cardboard, each 6 by 2 inches (15 by 5 centimeters). Poke a hole in one end of each piece. Center the holes to join these two pieces together with another brad.

Supplies

cardboard	white paint
ruler	paintbrush
scissors	markers
brads (fasteners with ends that bend)	

6 Poke a hole in the other end of each short piece. Join these pieces to the two long pieces with holes.

7 Paint the cardboard with white paint and decorate with markers to create your robotic arm. You can grab things with the closed end by holding the two open ends and moving them in and out.

Variation

EXPLORE WITH DIFFERENT SIZES OF MATERIAL. TRY JOINING MORE PIECES TOGETHER.

MAKE YOUR OWN!
ASTRONAUT ASTEROID TOOL BELT

During a space walk, astronauts have to wear a tool belt called an MMWS (modular mini-workstation). The MMWS wraps around the astronaut. It has tethers with clips that keep the tools from floating away.

1 Fold the fabric in half and secure the edges with a simple running stitch or fabric glue. Add buttons using glue to represent asteroids on your belt.

2 When the glue has dried, tie long pieces of yarn or string to some of the buttons. These represent the tethers used to keep astronauts' tools from floating off into space.

3 Braid together three pieces of yarn to create your belt fastener. It needs to be long enough to wrap around your waist.

Supplies

felt or scrap pieces of fabric long enough to be wrapped around your hips twice	needle and thread or fabric glue buttons yarn or string safety pins

4 You can secure the belt fastener to your tool belt with safety pins, so the yarn moves smoothly through them like belt loops on a pair of pants.

5 Tie the tool belt to your waist and you are ready for your next space mission.

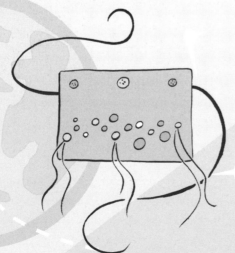

JUST FOR LAUGHS

Q What kind of belt doesn't go around your waist?

A An asteroid belt.

MAKE YOUR OWN!

WEARABLE SPACE SUIT

Why is a white space suit used for a spacewalk? How about purple or black? None of these colors would work. In the darkness of space white stands out the best. While you are going to wear your own clothes under your suit, an astronaut wears a special undergarment. This undergarment has tubes filled with water. The water is circulated with pumps to keep the astronaut cool and dry. Hands and feet are kept warm with heaters. Space suit design is constantly changing. What will your space suit look like?

Supplies

- newspaper
- paper paint suits from a hardware store
- paint and markers
- glitter (optional)

1 Spread newspaper out on the floor. Lay your paper paint suit on the newpaper.

2 Real space suits have a space badge, name patch, and country flag. Go to the Internet to see some pictures of astronauts in their space suits to get ideas.

3 Use your imagination and paint or draw your own amazing design. Add glitter to the paint if you like. Themes could include: objects in space, constellations, etc. If you are working in a group everyone could sign each other's costume. When the paint and glitter have dried, try on your suit. Ready, set, liftoff!

Variation FOR AN EARTH-FRIENDLY VERSION, HAVE A FRIEND TRACE YOUR UPPER TORSO ONTO A LARGE PIECE OF RECYCLED PAPER. DO BOTH FRONT AND BACK. CONNECT THE TWO PIECES WITH STRING. DECORATE THE PIECES AND SLIP YOUR SPACESUIT OVER YOUR HEAD.

MAKE YOUR OWN!

ASTRONAUT EMERGENCY GAME

Physical training is an important part of astronaut training. Astronauts have to be able to run and do a variety of tasks in their space suits. The fitter they are, the better they can perform. See if you have what it takes to step aboard a spacecraft.

Supplies

group of players

astronaut suits, boots, tool belts, and gloves for each player

1 Divide into two evenly sized groups. Each team will need astronaut suits, boots, and gloves arranged into separate piles.

2 The first player of each team dresses quickly in astronaut gear, runs to a designated spot and runs back to his or her team.

3 The player tags the next person, and then sits down to show that they have boarded the shuttle.

4 The first team to get all their astronauts dressed and sitting down flies the shuttle. The other team is ground control.

Variation

HAVE ONE COMPLETE SUIT PER TEAM. EACH PLAYER HAS TO PUT ON THE SUIT, RUN, AND REMOVE THE SUIT FOR THE NEXT PLAYER.

MEET THE NEIGHBORS: THE PLANETS

Have you ever made a map? Ancient astronomers did. They mapped the night sky. It was just as exciting then as it is today. Astronomers realized stars moved in fixed patterns. We call these patterns **constellations**. A few stars were different—they wandered. We call these wandering stars **planets**. *Planet* is a Greek word meaning "wanderer."

The Greeks named the five visible planets that they knew about after their **gods**. Greek names were given to the other planets later, when they were discovered.

I WANNA CALL THIS ONE NEPTUNE!

We know the seven other planets in our solar system (besides earth) by their Latin names. They are Mercury, Venus, Mars, Jupiter, Saturn, Uranus, and Neptune. Unlike stars, planets do change their positions. This is because planets orbit the sun. It's easy to see five of the planets. And all of the planets travel closer to Earth than stars.

Some cultures believed the wandering stars were gods. It wasn't until 1610 that people realized planets were worlds. And who was responsible for this shocking discovery? Why Galileo and his telescope of course!

WORDS 2 KNOW

constellation: a group of stars visible within a particular region of the night sky that form a pattern.

planet: a body in space that orbits the sun and does not produce its own light.

gods: beings that are worshipped and believed to have special powers.

space probe: a spacecraft that explores the solar system and sends data back to Earth.

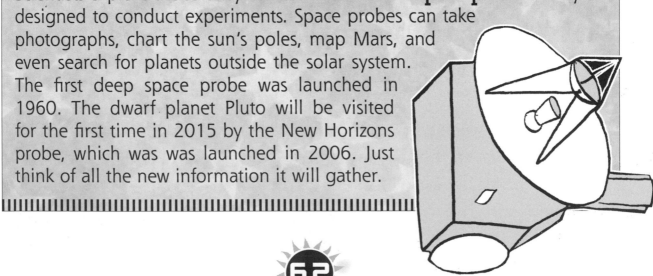

Space Probes

Scientists explore the solar system with unmanned **space probes**. They're designed to conduct experiments. Space probes can take photographs, chart the sun's poles, map Mars, and even search for planets outside the solar system. The first deep space probe was launched in 1960. The dwarf planet Pluto will be visited for the first time in 2015 by the New Horizons probe, which was was launched in 2006. Just think of all the new information it will gather.

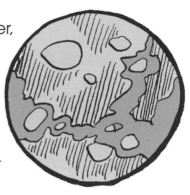

In 1781 William Herschel, an English astronomer, thought he was looking at a comet. Later it was found to be a planet. This planet was called Uranus. Neptune was discovered in 1846.

With modern telescopes astronomers can look even deeper into space. We can only imagine what still waits to be discovered.

TERRESTRIAL PLANETS

The planets in our solar system can be divided into two groups. The first group, closest to the sun, are the terrestrial planets. *Terrestrial* means, "earth-like." The terrestrial planets are Mercury, Venus, Earth, and Mars. They all have rocky surfaces. The heat from the sun melted the ice and frozen gases of these planets. This is why terrestrial planets have surfaces of hard rock with a core of metal. Venus, Earth, and Mars all have atmospheres. Mercury doesn't have an atmosphere. Terrestrial planets are similar to each other in size.

Mercury is the closest planet to the sun.

•Mercury was the messenger of the gods in Roman mythology.

•Mercury does not have an atmosphere because its gravity is too weak.

•The first space probe to visit Mercury was Mariner 10 in 1974–75.

•Mercury travels around the sun quickly compared to other planets, but it spins slowly. So a day on Mercury is longer than a year!

•It's hard to see Mercury from Earth because it's so close to the sun. Look for Mercury just before sunrise and sunset within a few degrees of the sun.

Venus is the second-closest planet to the sun.

•The surface of Venus is like something out of a horror movie. Thick cloud cover traps the sun's heat, making temperatures on the surface soar to 870 degrees Fahrenheit (465 degrees Celsius).

•The air pressure on Venus would crush you. It's 90 times greater than the pressure of the air on Earth.

•To see Venus, look for the brightest object in the sky. In the early morning and early evening during a crescent moon, it will be near the moon.

•The first probe to land on Venus was Venera 7. It relayed data for less than 30 minutes before burning up in the scorching heat.

Mars is the fourth planet from the sun.

•Mars was the Roman god of war.

•It's sometimes called the red planet because its surface is a reddish color.

•Mars rotates every 24 hours, 39 minutes, close to the length of Earth's rotation.

•It has two moons, named Phobos and Deimos.

•Mars has the largest volcano in the solar system, called Olympus Mons.

•NASA's Mars rovers, Spirit and Opportunity, have been exploring Mars since early 2004. By 2009 they had sent back over 250,000 photos! You can see some of these photos on NASA's web site.

THEN AND NOW FACTOID

then: Galileo was the first person to see the rings of Saturn. He thought the rings might be moons.

now: We know the rings of Saturn are bits of ice and rock. They may be from a moon that moved too close to the planet.

JOVIAN PLANETS

Located just beyond the orbit of Mars, a belt of asteroids divides the terrestrial planets from the Jovian planets. Jovian means the planets in this group all have characteristics similar to Jupiter. They are Jupiter, Saturn, Uranus, and Neptune.

Unlike terrestrial planets, Jovian planets formed farther away from the sun. These planets do not have hard surfaces. You wouldn't go for a stroll on any of them. These planets are made of various gases. The

JUST FOR LAUGHS

Q What do you get when you put eight bodies together?

A The solar system.

principal gases are hydrogen and helium. Their cores are thought to be made of ice and rock.

All Jovian planets have rings. Saturn's are best known because they are most easily seen. Another characteristic of Jovian planets is that they all have a lot of moons. Saturn has 60, Jupiter has 63, Uranus has 27, and Neptune has 13. With new telescopes and space missions, astronomers may find even more moons.

Pluto

Pluto lies beyond Neptune. It used to be called a planet. Then in 2006 scientists decided it should be grouped with other small planets in the outer solar system and called a dwarf planet. Pluto's orbit overlaps Neptune's every 248 years. It was discovered in 1930 and named for the Roman god of the dead. With its three moons, Pluto takes 200 years to orbit the sun. One Plutonian year equals 248 Earth years! Pluto is one of the coldest places in the solar system.

Jovian planets are huge compared to the terrestrial planets. Jupiter is 11 times bigger than Earth, Saturn is 9 times bigger, and Uranus and Neptune are 4 times larger. Despite their size, they are not dense because they are made of gas. Saturn is made of materials lighter than water. If you could place Saturn in an enormous swimming pool, it would float!

OUT OF THIS WORLD

Venus is the only planet where the sun rises in the west and sets in the east. This is because, unlike other planets, Venus rotates in the opposite direction of its orbit.

WOW!

Jupiter is the fifth planet from the sun.

•Jupiter was the Roman king of the gods.

•It's the largest planet in the solar system.

•Over 1,000 Earths could fit inside Jupiter.

•Jupiter's great red spot is a giant storm believed to have been in existence for 300 years. Three Earths would fit across it!

•Jupiter takes 11.9 Earth years to orbit around the sun.

•Galileo was the first to see the moons of Jupiter.

Saturn is the sixth planet from the sun.

•Saturn is the most distant planet we can see with the naked eye.

•The Cassini-Huygens mission entered Saturn's orbit in 2004. The Huygens probe dropped into the atmosphere of Saturn's moon, Titan.

•In mythology, Saturn was the god of agriculture.

•It takes Saturn nearly 30 years to circle the sun.

•Saturn's thousands of rings are made of rock and ice.

DWARF PLANETS

In 2006 the International Astronomical Union developed a new way of classifying planets. It was suspected that many objects similar to Pluto would be discovered in the future, so a new category was created. Objects In this category are called dwarf planets. A dwarf planet is a small planet in the outer solar system that orbits the sun. The dwarf planets include Ceres, Pluto, Eris, MakeMake, and Haumea. There are already dozens of dwarf planets that have been discovered!

Uranus is the seventh planet from the sun.

•Uranus (pronounced yúr-e-nes) takes a little more than 84 years to circle the sun.

•In Greek mythology, Uranus was the god of the heavens.

•Uranus spins on its side.

•The Voyager 2 probe flew by Uranus in 1986. It recorded lightning crashing in the atmosphere.

Neptune is the eighth planet from the sun.

•In Roman mythology, Neptune was the god of the sea.

•Neptune is the smallest of the gas giants.

•Winds on Neptune are the fastest in the solar system, clocking in at 1,200 miles per hour (2,000 kilometers per hour)!

•The only probe to have ever flown near Neptune was Voyager 2 in 1989.

•It takes Neptune almost 165 years to orbit the sun. This means that since its discovery in 1846, Neptune has not yet completed one full orbit! This won't happen until 2011.

Space Firsts

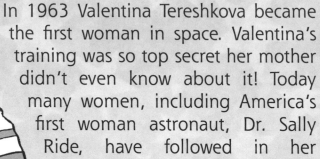

SPACE

In 1963 Valentina Tereshkova became the first woman in space. Valentina's training was so top secret her mother didn't even know about it! Today many women, including America's first woman astronaut, Dr. Sally Ride, have followed in her footsteps. Women walk in space, command space shuttles, and work assembling space stations.

STAR PLAYER

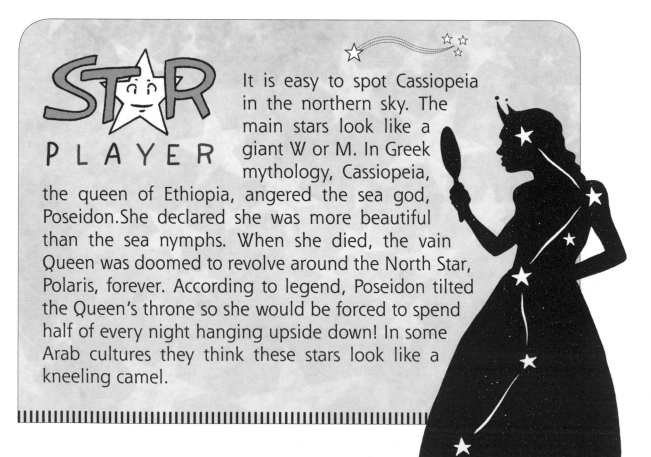

It is easy to spot Cassiopeia in the northern sky. The main stars look like a giant W or M. In Greek mythology, Cassiopeia, the queen of Ethiopia, angered the sea god, Poseidon. She declared she was more beautiful than the sea nymphs. When she died, the vain Queen was doomed to revolve around the North Star, Polaris, forever. According to legend, Poseidon tilted the Queen's throne so she would be forced to spend half of every night hanging upside down! In some Arab cultures they think these stars look like a kneeling camel.

SHH....IT'S A SECRET

Binary code is a number code people can use to talk to machines. Binary numbers are used to represent all information in the digital world using 0 and 1. The letter A is 01000001 and B is 01000010. Spacecraft such as Voyager use binary code to send information back to Earth. Even photographs can be transmitted this way!

Would you like to send a secret message? Here's a simpler version that you and a friend can use. In this code each letter of the alphabet is represented by a number. Use this chart to help you.

A	B	C	D	E	F	G	H	I	J	K	L	M	N	O	P	Q	R	S	T	U	V	W	X	Y	Z
1	2	3	4	5	6	7	8	9	10	11	12	13	14	15	16	17	18	19	20	21	22	23	24	25	26

See if you can decode this message from a famous astronaut.

15-14-5   19-13-1-12-12   19-20-5-16   6-15-18   13-1-14   15-14-5

7-9-1-14-20   12-5-1-16   6-15-18   13-1-14-11-9-14-4

Johannes Kepler

Johannes Kepler (1571–1630) was born in Germany. He was an excellent student. Johannes worked out how the planets moved. He realized the planets moved in elliptical orbits around the sun. Johannes helped astronomers to work out distances from the planets to the sun.

MAKE YOUR OWN!

RINGS OF SATURN WHIRLIGIG

Saturn's rings stretch around its diameter. They are not solid like a ring you would wear. They are bits of ice and rock. Gravity holds the pieces together. The rings cover a distance almost equal to the distance from the earth to the moon! Now you can recreate the famous rings of Saturn with paint and paper.

Supplies

thick elastic bands	white glue
cardboard	paint
scissors	hole puncher
	yarn or string

1 Cut pieces of an elastic band into interesting shapes and glue them to small cardboard squares. These squares will become the stamps used to create the rings.

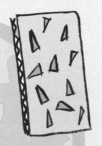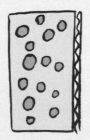

2 When the glue has dried, dip your stamps into the paint and create patterns on a larger piece of cardboard. Overlap your designs to create more texture.

3 Allow the paint to dry, then cut out different sized circles. Punch a hole through center of one of the circles.

4 Cut a two-foot length of yarn and thread it through the hole. Hold the yarn taut and spin your whirligig. Watch as the colors blend together.

Tip USE DIFFERENT SIZED CIRCLES AND VARY YARN LENGTH TO CREATE MORE RINGS.

MAKE YOUR OWN! SPACE PROBE

Space probes send information to Earth from millions of miles away. The data they send back might one day be used to build a Mars colony! Today you can build and fly your space probe anywhere in the solar system. What will your probe tell scientists?

1 Cover the box with foil and place to one side. Create two solar panels from card stock in proportion to the box and cover with foil.

2 Attach a solar panel to each side of the box with tape. Now assemble the communication tower by placing the plate face down on the box and the bowl face up on the plate.

3 Attach the communication tower by pushing two pins through the plate, bowl, and into the box. You may need to secure this with tape.

Supplies

small box such as a sunscreen container	paper plate
	long straight pins
	pipe cleaners
aluminum foil	styrofoam balls
recycled card stock	glue
Scotch tape	buttons and/or beads
paper bowl	

4 Twist the pipe cleaner and attach it to the bowl. Attach two Styrofoam balls to one another with a pin and use a second pin to secure them onto the plate's rim.

5 Decorate your probe with small objects such as buttons or beads.

Hint USING STRAIGHT PINS ALLOWS YOUR COMMUNICATION TOWER TO TWIST AND TURN. IF YOU PREFER TO USE GLUE FOR A MORE STABLE PROJECT, GO AHEAD.

MAKE YOUR OWN!

MARS ROVER

Bouncing along the surface of Mars are two NASA robots: Spirit and Opportunity. They landed on Mars in 2004. The rovers are searching for evidence that water existed on Mars in the past. Their original mission was for only 90 days. Dust storms and Martian winters threaten to freeze the rovers, but they are still going. Don't you think that's incredible? Check the NASA web site www.marsrovers.jpl.nasa.gov to find out what Spirit and Opportunity are up to. What will you name your Mars rover?

1 Cut each hanger one inch down from the hook on both sides. Cut the bottom of the hangers in half. Use the mallet and the discarded hook to pierce the end of one of the cans. You may need an adult's help.

2 Push one hanger through the can and position the can halfway along the bottom part of the wire. Use the pliers to bend the wire up so the can "wheel" does not come off the wire.

3 Use tape to attach the hanger to the cereal box. You might need to bend the hanger wire so it fits snugly around the box. Make certain the can "wheel" can move. Repeat with all five cans.

Supplies

3 wire coat hangers	tape
wire cutters	cereal box
mallet	tissue or other colorful paper
6 small cans	
needle-nose pliers	glue or Mod Podge

4 Now you are ready to decorate your Mars rover. Use glue that dries clear or Mod Podge and bits of newspaper, colorful fliers, magazines, or tissue paper. Wait for the glue to dry before you take your rover for a spin.

Tip MAKE SURE AN ADULT FINDS SIX CANS WITH NO SHARP EDGES. SODA OR JUICE CANS WORK WELL. YOU CAN USE PIPE CLEANERS TO ADD A ROBOTIC ARM AND CAMERA TO YOU ROVER.

ASTEROIDS, METEORS & COMETS

*E*xtra, extra, read all about it. Visitors from outer space have reached Earth! They traveled millions of miles until their journey intersected with ours. What did they look like? Well, they weren't green. Some left behind giant craters. Others appeared as moving white lights in the sky. What could they be?

☆ ✶ ☆ ⭐ ☆ ✦ ☆ ⭐ ☆ ✩

Not all bodies in space are as massive as planets. There are smaller objects that orbit the sun. They are called meteors, comets, and asteroids. Made from rock or ice, these objects begin their journey deep in the solar system. On a clear night, look up. You might see these visitors from outer space.

ASTEROIDS

Hundreds and thousands of boulders tumble through space. They are asteroids. The word *asteroid* in Greek means "like a star." Asteroids are fragments of rock and metal, shaped like potatoes or peanuts. There is even one asteroid that looks like a dog's bone! Why are asteroids so oddly shaped? Because their gravity is too low to pull them into a round shape.

Most asteroids are found in the **asteroid belt**. This is a 20-million-mile area of space located between Mars and Jupiter. The asteroid belt is like a dividing line in space. It separates the inner planets from the outer planets. Other asteroids orbit close to the sun, and some have been captured by the gravity of the planets.

asteroid belt: a region in space between Mars and Jupiter that contains many asteroids.

meteor: a small rocky or metallic body orbiting the sun.

Scientists aren't certain how asteroids formed. They are probably leftovers from when the solar system was created. Asteroids range in size from tiny chunks to pieces hundreds of miles (kilometers) wide. Their surfaces are cratered, showing a history of random collisions, as if they were floating bumper cars. Ceres is the largest and first asteroid ever found. It is 584 miles (940

OUT OF THIS WORLD

Comet Hyakutake has the longest tail ever recorded. The tail stretched for more than 354 million miles (570 million kilometers) away from the sun. WOW!

Draco, or the Dragon, winds its way around the Little Dipper like a serpent. It is so far north that it is always visible over the horizon in North America, although it can be hard to find. Draco is the eighth-largest constellation in the heavens. In Roman mythology, the dragon guarded golden apples in a heavenly garden.

kilometers) in diameter. It was discovered by Giuseppi Piazzi in 1801. Now Ceres is considered a dwarf planet. Since its discovery in 1801, over 100,000 asteroids have been classified. But even if all the asteroids were put together, their mass would still be less than that of the moon.

METEORS

Meteors are small particles of matter in the solar system. The word *meteor* comes from the Greek word *meteoron*, which means "high in the air." Meteors are sometimes called shooting or falling stars. But meteors are not stars. They

are small fragments of rock and mineral. Some meteors are asteroids that got bumped out of their orbit. As meteors burn up in Earth's atmosphere, they look like streaks of light in the night sky. Thousands enter Earth's atmosphere daily.

Meteor Showers

Meteor showers occur when Earth passes through a dead comet. Meteor showers are like streaks of light flashing across the night sky.

Most meteors are burned up by the intense heat in our atmosphere. Very few ever make it to Earth's surface. If they crash into the surface of Earth they are called meteorites. Meteorites are named for where they fall or where they are found. There are hundreds of meteorite craters on Earth. Over 25,000 meteorites have been found around the world. And 18,000 are from Antarctica! They are easy to find in the snow.

Spot a Meteor

On a clear evening, dress for the weather, bring a folding lawn chair outside, and look up. You might need insect repellent in some parts of North America. Meteors can appear anywhere in the sky. You don't need a telescope or binoculars, but you do need to be in a dark place far from city lights. The best time to look is between midnight and dawn, but you will often see them any time after dark. If you see a bright light streak across the sky, you've spotted a meteor!

COMETS

Comets are like dirty snow balls. They are a combination of dust and icy water. The word *comet* comes from the Greek word *kome* meaning "hair." A comet's long tail must have reminded the Greeks of hair.

When a comet nears the sun, it begins to vaporize. This causes the comet to develop a bright tail. A comet's tail can be over 10 million miles (16 million kilometers) long. Some comets have two tails. One tail is gas and another is dust.

Long ago, the arrival of a comet was greeted with fear. Comets were thought to be

JUST FOR LAUGHS

Q Which celestial body is not a vegetarian?

A A meteor.

comet: a ball of rocks, ice, and dirt that orbits the sun.

Kuiper belt: a region of space beyond the planets in our solar system containing many asteroids and dwarf planets.

Oort cloud: a collection of a huge number of comets that orbit around the outer reaches of the solar system.

a sign of some future disaster. The word *disaster* comes from the Latin *aster*, meaning "star." Comets were blamed for failed battles, disease, and earthquakes. This is not true, only superstition. A superstition is a belief not based on fact.

Like planets, comets orbit the sun. Unlike planets, their orbits can be extremely long and skinny ellipses. Halley's comet is a famous comet, well documented in history. Its orbit is 76 years long. It's scheduled to pass by Earth again in 2062. The length of a comet's orbit depends on where in the solar system it came from.

Space First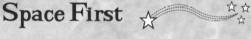

In 1972, Pioneer 10 became the first spacecraft to make it through the asteroid belt. A little over 10 years later it became the first probe to leave the solar system. On the probe are plaques with illustrations of humans and Earth's location in the galaxy. Do you think a space civilization will one day read them?

Meteor Crater Pudding

To make an edible, meteor crater pudding, ask an adult to open a can of pudding. Smooth the pudding into a shallow dish. Put together a selection of candy in different weights and sizes. Meteorites come in various sizes and shapes. Drop the candy into the pudding. You can compare the sizes of the different craters and eat the end results!

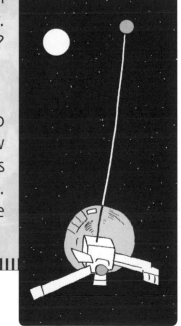

Caroline Herschel

Caroline Herschel (1750–1848) was the first woman to discover a comet. She assisted her brother William with his work in astronomy. William discovered the planet Uranus. When he gave Caroline a telescope of her own, she discovered her first comet. That was on August 1, 1786. The king of England made Caroline the assistant to the court astronomer. Caroline discovered seven more comets.

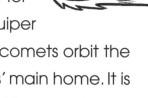

Comets originate in the **Kuiper belt** and the **Oort cloud**. Both areas are named for Dutch astronomers. Comets from the Kuiper belt are called short-period comets. These comets orbit the sun in less than 200 years. The Oort cloud is the comets' main home. It is 100,000 AUs from the sun. That is 5 trillion miles (9 trillion kilometers) from the sun! This area is home to long-period comets. They take a much longer time to orbit the sun.

Over 850 comets have been found. It is thought comets have not changed since the creation of the solar system. Space probes are now used to investigate comets. The information gathered helps scientists learn more about the solar system.

then: Halley's comet was blamed for England's defeat at the Battle of Hastings in 1066. It was seen in the skies at that time and embroidered on a tapestry. The famous Bayeux tapestry can be seen in a museum in Bayeux, France.

now: Halley's comet is named for Edmund Halley. He suggested comets regularly return to Earth's orbit. Comets are an important part of our history.

MAKE YOUR OWN! SHOOTING COMET WHEEL

Turn the wheel to follow a comet's orbit around the sun. Comets form a bright tail when they near the sun, as gas and dust are forced away by the sun's heat. A comet's tail always points away from the sun.

1 Cut a square larger than your ellipse template out of the paper or card stock.

2 Tace your ellipse template onto the square. Near the left edge of the ellipse draw a sun.

3 Use a hole punch to make holes less than half an inch apart around the ellipse. Put this paper to one side.

4 Cut out a circle slightly larger than the square. Find the center and draw a faint line from the center to one edge.

5 To represent the comet's tail, divide the line into three equal sections.

Supplies

scissors	pencil
construction paper or card paper	hole punch
ellipse template	brad

6 Color the comet's tail so the section nearest the center is the brightest and the color slowly fades out.

7 Line up the centers of the square and circle and push a brad through. The layers should be able to spin freely.

8 Now you are ready to spin your comet.

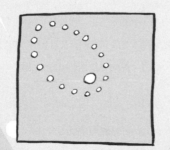

OBSERVE HOW THE LIGHT GETS STRONGER NEARER THE SUN AND IS FAINTER AS THE COMET MOVES AWAY.

MAKE YOUR OWN!

METEOR SHOWER SNOWGLOBE

Meteor showers come from comets. Dust particles that cause a meteor shower are leftover debris from comets. When a comet flies close to the sun, the sun's heat melts the comet's icy surface. This leaves behind a cloud of dust. When even a little of this dust hits Earth's atmosphere it disintegrates in a bright flash of light. We call this a meteor!

1 Cut out a piece of acetate large enough to fit inside your jar. Use markers to create a night sky picture on the acetate, complete with your favorite constellations and a comet.

2 Curl the acetate into an "S" shape and place it in the jar. Fill the jar three-quarters full with water, and add a tablespoon of glycerin to thicken it.

3 Add a thick layer of glitter (you can make some by crushing eggshells).

4 Close your jar's lid, and seal it with modeling clay to make it watertight.

5 Using construction paper cut strips to frame a window. Glue your window onto the jar and let dry.

6 Shake the jar, look through the window, and watch a comet shoot by.

Variation: ADD FIGURINES SUCH AS A MINIATURE HOUSE, ANIMALS, OR TREES AND SECURE THESE INSIDE THE LID WITH STRONG, WATER-SOLUBLE GLUE.

Supplies

small clear jar with a screw-top lid	glycerin
acetate fabric	glitter, sparkles, or crushed egg shells
scissors	modeling clay
colored permanent markers	construction paper
water	glue

MAKE YOUR OWN! EDIBLE COMET

Comets originate in the outer regions of the solar system but you can create one in your own kitchen. Invite some friends over to eat a frozen relic from the formation of the solar system.

TIP TRY TO WORK QUICKLY OR YOUR COMET WILL DISAPPEAR BEFORE YOUR FIRST BITE.

Supplies

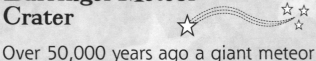

ice cubes	evaporated milk
blender	chocolate wafers or shaved chocolate
desert bowl	
syrup or fruit juice	marshmallow cream

1 Ask an adult to finely chop a dozen ice cubes in a blender. When the ice is crushed, place a portion into a bowl.

2 Pour a little syrup or fruit juice over the ice and mold it into a ball. Next add a spoonful of evaporated milk to turn the ice into snow.

3 Crumble a chocolate wafer and sprinkle it over the snowball to represent the dirt in a comet. Use marshmallow cream for the comet's tail.

4 Now your comet is ready to share with a friend or enjoy by yourself.

Variation YOU CAN MAKE A COLORFUL COMET BY ADDING DIFFERENT COLORED SYRUPS OR FRUIT TOPPINGS.

Barringer Meteor Crater

Over 50,000 years ago a giant meteor slammed into an area near Winslow, Arizona. It vaporized an area 4,100 feet (1,249 meters) in diameter and 570 feet (173 meters) deep. Some boulders spit up by the meteor's impact are the size of a small home. The area was used by NASA as a training site for the Apollo astronauts.

STAR LIGHT, STAR BRIGHT

Star light. Star bright. Look at the sky tonight. Has someone sprinkled silver glitter in the sky? No, it's not glitter. Those sparkling points of light are stars. They are always in the sky, day or night. It's just easier to see them when it's dark.

☆ ✲ ☆ ★ ☆ ✲ ★ ☆ ☆ ✶

The stars are not part of our solar system. They do not orbit the sun, our star. But they are so important in our night sky that we're going to learn about them here.

When you gaze at the sky you see only a small portion of the stars in the universe. The human eye can see only about 2,000 stars. But there are billions of stars, more than all the grains of sand in all the beaches. You could spend your entire life counting the stars and never finish!

82

Our sun is an average-sized star. There are larger and hotter stars. There are also cooler and smaller stars. But all stars are balls of gas. Stars are born in **nebulas**. Nebulas are great masses of dust and gas.

A star begins to shine when it produces its own heat and light. The sun is the brightest star we see because it is the closest to Earth.

When a star like our sun begins to run out of fuel it glows red as it cools. These stars are called red giants. As the star continues to cool it glows white, earning it the name white dwarf. When the star is no longer glowing it becomes a black dwarf. Stars live for millions and millions of years. Some can live for 100 billion years.

Stardust

Do you have stars in your eyes? The answer is yes. All the **atoms** in your body except hydrogen are made from stars. An atom is a tiny building block. When stars die, new stars are created. This is how the sun was born. The sun made life possible on Earth. And that's why you're made of stardust.

CONSTELLATIONS

Looking at stars is exciting. Have you ever tried to join the dots of light together? Well, many ancient astronomers did. Around the globe people gazed at the stars and grouped them into patterns and pictures. It's a dog. It's a swan. These pictures in the sky are called constellations. One of the oldest paintings of the constellations was found in a cave in France. The cave painting shows the night sky as it appeared over 17,000 years ago!

TAURUS

PERSEUS

ARIES

JUST FOR LAUGHS

Q What do you call a star that's edible?

A A star fruit.

Ancient people told stories about the stars. The sky was like a giant picture book with the characters illuminated in lights. Every culture gave names to the stars. Stars in the same constellation aren't really close, though. Hundreds of **light years** separate them.

Stars have many names. This is because they were observed and grouped by different cultures. Many of the constellation names we use in North America were given by Greek and Roman astronomers. Today you will find a mix of these names as well as other patterns observed by later astronomers. Other constellations were named in the fifteenth and sixteenth centuries by sailors. When European sailors made their way to the Southern Hemisphere they saw constellations no European had ever seen before. No European had looked at the stars from the Southern Hemisphere until then!

If you live on the equator you can view all the constellations in a year! Today, there are 88 commonly recognized constellations.

STAR PLAYER

Ursa Major, or the Great Bear, is a constellation that has seven bright stars. The Algonquin Indians told their children a story about a strong bear that terrorized their villages. Hunters chased the bear, who escaped by running up into the sky. A group of stars within Ursa Major are today known as the Big Dipper. The Big Dipper is one of the most recognizable constellations in the night sky.

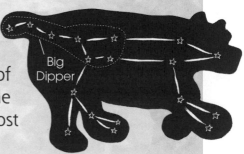

Big Dipper

MILKY WAY

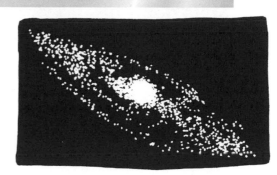

The stars you see are part of our galaxy, the Milky Way. Galaxies are collections of gas, dust, and stars. The word *galaxy* comes from the Greek word for milk. The Milky Way is a strip of white stretching across the night sky.

The white strip is millions of stars. Everything that we can see in the sky is part of the Milky Way. This includes comets, asteroids, moons, and planets. If you could stand outside our galaxy in space and look back at our galaxy, it would look like a giant, twirling carnival ride. Earth is located on one of the giant spinning arms. It would take light 100,000 years to cross our galaxy. It takes the sun about 225 million years to orbit the center of the Milky Way!

The Milky Way galaxy is only one of many galaxies in the universe. Scientists believe there are hundreds of billions of galaxies. Some are like ours and others are different. There are three major types, with names that describe their shape: spiral galaxy, elliptical galaxy, and irregular galaxy. Each galaxy is home to hundreds of billions of stars. Between the galaxies is relatively empty space.

nebula: a giant cloud of gas and dust among the stars.

atoms: small particles in the universe that make up everything. Atoms are like tiny building blocks, like grains of sand.

light years: a unit of measure for very long distances.

MAKE YOUR OWN! ¡TRAVEL WITH THE STARS! GAME

Stars don't disappear during the day. It's just easier to see them at night. With this game they'll always be in the palm of your hand. Using the buttons as stars, make a constellation on the tin. See if a friend can correctly identify it. Take turns. As you learn more constellations make more button stars.

Supplies

tin container with a wide bottom	paintbrush
sandpaper	white glue
cloth rag or paper towel	scissors
paint, any color	magazine scraps
	buttons
	magnet strips

1 Rub sandpaper all over the tin container. Wipe off the grit. Sanding the tin container will help make the paint stick.

2 Paint the container and let dry. Cut out magazine scraps to decorate the sides of the container. Glue the pieces onto the sides.

3 Cut pieces of magnet that are smaller than the buttons. Glue a piece of the strip magnet onto each button, for 12 in all. These are your stars.

4 Now arrange the buttons in the shapes of constellations and have a friend guess which constellation it is.

Variation
MATCH THE CONSTELLATION WITH A MAGNET PRINTED WITH ITS CORRESPONDING NAME.

JUST for LAUGHS

Q Why did the star go to the grocery store?

A It was looking for the Milky Way.

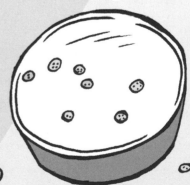

MAKE YOUR OWN!

MINI PLANETARIUM

A planetarium creates the illusion of a night sky. With your mini planetarium the stars will light up just about any dark room.

1 Lightly draw a few different constellations of your choice on the paper cups. Poke holes for stars.

2 Arrange the cups in a circle. Shine the flashlight on the cups and turn off the lights.

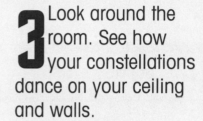

3 Look around the room. See how your constellations dance on your ceiling and walls.

Supplies

paper cups
sharp pencil
flashlight

Variation

SOME STARS APPEAR BRIGHTER THAN OTHERS BECAUSE THEY ARE AT DIFFERENT DISTANCES FROM EARTH. TRY THIS WITH A GROUP OF FRIENDS. EACH PERSON WILL NEED A FLASHLIGHT. WHEN THE SUN GOES DOWN INSTRUCT YOUR FRIENDS TO STAND AT DIFFERENT DISTANCES FROM YOU. THEN HAVE EVERYONE TURN ON THEIR FLASHLIGHT. WHAT DO YOU NOTICE?

FOCUS ON

Edwin Hubble

Edwin Hubble (1889–1953) was an American astronomer who made a system for classifying galaxies. Did you know the universe is expanding? Well, Edwin Hubble discovered that galaxies are slowly moving away from each other. The Hubble Space Telescope is named for him. This telescope is the size of a school bus and is the largest telescope ever launched into space. Since 1990 the Hubble has accomplished many firsts. Orbiting Earth, it sends back amazing photographs. Thanks to the Hubble, astronomers can see even more stars.

MAKE YOUR OWN!
CONSTELLATION SHADOW PUPPETS

Constellations were associated with popular tales about vain queens, two-headed monsters, and much more. You can create constellation puppets to act out some of these ancient stories.

Supplies

black construction paper	popsicle sticks or twigs
pencil	glue
white chalk	white sheet
scissors	string
	desk light

1 Choose a few of your favorite constellations from previous chapters.

2 Draw their shapes using white chalk, and lightly join the stars to form your constellation. You can color the major stars a little darker.

3 Carefully cut out your constellations. Glue a popsicle stick on the back of each, leaving room for a handle.

4 String up a white sheet by tying it to two chairs, and dim the lights.

5 Shine the desk light at the sheet from behind. You are now ready for your constellation puppet show to begin. Act out myths associated with the constellations with a group of friends.

OUT OF THIS WORLD

The three pyramids at Giza in northern Egypt seem to be aligned with Orion's belt. It was believed the stars could guide the dead pharaoh. Egyptians associated these stars with the god of death, Osiris.
WOW!

asteroid belt: a region in space between Mars and Jupiter that contains many asteroids.

asteroid: a small, rocky object that orbits the sun.

astronaut: a person who travels or works in space.

astronomer: a person who studies the stars, planets, and other bodies in space.

astronomical unit: a unit of measure used in space. The average distance from the earth to the sun, 93 million miles.

atmosphere: the mixture of gases surrounding a planet.

atoms: small particles in the universe that make up everything, like tiny building blocks or grains of sand.

aurora australis: colored lights in the sky around the South Pole.

aurora borealis: colored lights in the sky around the North Pole.

aurora: visible colored light in the night sky around the North and South Poles.

Big Bang: the explosion that many scientists think started the universe.

comet: a ball of rocks, ice, and dirt that orbits the sun.

constellation: a group of stars visible in the night sky that form a pattern.

continent: a large landmass rising high in the earth's crust.

convex: a rounded shape like the outside of a bowl.

core: iron-rich center of the earth.

corona: the outermost part of the sun's atmosphere.

crater: a large bowl-shaped hole in the ground caused by an asteroid's impact.

crescent moon: when less than half of the moon is showing.

crust: Earth's outermost layer.

dwarf planet: a small planet in the outer solar system.

ellipse: an oval shape.

far side of the moon: the side of the moon that faces away from Earth.

fossil fuels: fuel made from the remains of ancient plants and animals.

full moon: when the whole moon shows.

fuse: join together.

galaxy: a collection of star systems held together by gravity.

global warming: an increase in Earth's temperatures.

gods: beings that are worshipped and believed to have special powers.

gravity: the force that pulls objects toward each other.

greenhouse gases: gases that contribute to the warming of Earth's atmosphere.

helium: a colorless gas created in a nuclear reaction in the sun.

hydrogen: a colorless gas that is the most abundant gas in the universe.

Jovian planet: one of the planets made mostly of gas—Jupiter, Saturn, Uranus, Neptune.

Kuiper belt: a region of space beyond the planets in our solar system containing many asteroids and dwarf planets.

light year: unit of measure for very long distances.

lunar cycle: the moon's phases, from crescent moon to full moon and back again.

lunar eclipse: the earth passing between the sun and the moon, casting a shadow on the moon.

lunar month: the period between the beginning and end of the moon's cycle.

mantle: the layer of the earth between the crust and core.

maria: lowland seas.

meteor: a small, rocky, or metallic body orbiting the sun. Also the streak of light from a meteoroid hitting the earth's atmosphere.

meteorite: a piece of meteoroid that has landed on a planet or moon.

meteoroid: a rock that orbits the sun. Smaller than an asteroid.

microgravity: very low gravity.

Milky Way: the galaxy where our solar system is located.

mission control: a command center on Earth that helps astronauts on their mission.

moon: a body that orbits a planet.

NASA: National Aeronautics and Space Administration. The U.S. organization in charge of space exploration.

nebula: a giant cloud of gas and dust among the stars.

nuclear reaction: when atoms fuse or split apart, releasing a large amount of energy.

Northern Hemisphere: the part of the earth north of the equator.

observatory: a place from which astronomers can observe the planets, stars, and galaxies.

Oort cloud: a huge collection of comets that orbit around the outer regions of the solar system.

orbit: the path of an object circling another object in space.

ozone layer: the layer of the earth's atmosphere that contains ozone and blocks the sun's ultraviolet rays.

particle: tiny piece of something.

patent: when an invention is protected from illegal copying.

phases: the changing appearance of the moon during a month.

philosopher: someone who thinks about and questions the way things are in the world.

photosphere: the brightest, most visible layer of a star, what we see as the surface.

planet: a large body in space that orbits the sun and does not produce its own light. There are eight planets.

probe: a spaceship or satellite used to explore outer space.

prominence: a stream or loop of gas on the sun.

Proxima Centauri: the second-nearest star to Earth.

reflecting telescope: a telescope that uses a curved mirror to collect light.

refracting telescope: a telescope with a lens that gathers light and forms an image of something far away.

rotation: turning all the way around.

satellite: an object that orbits the earth, or that orbits the sun or another planet.

solar core: the center of the sun, where it produces its energy.

solar eclipse: when the moon moves between the sun and the earth, blocking the sun's light.

solar flare: a sudden burst of energy from the sun's surface.

solar system: the collection of eight planets and their moons in orbit around the sun, together with smaller bodies in the form of asteroids, meteoroids, comets, and dwarf planets.

solar wind: the flow of many tons of tiny particles from the sun's surface into space each second.

Southern Hemisphere: the part of the earth south of the equator.

Soviet Union: a former country that included present-day Russia.

space probe: a spacecraft that explores the solar system and sends data back to Earth.

space race: the race between countries to successfully land an astronaut on the moon.

species: a type of animal or plant.

spyglass: a telescope small enough to hold in your hands.

summer solstice: the longest day of the year. June 21 in the Northern Hemisphere.

sunspot: a dark area on the sun's surface that is cooler than the surrounding area.

tectonic plates: moving pieces of the earth's crust.

telescope: a tool used to see objects that are far away.

terrestrial planet: a rocky planet like Mercury, Venus, Earth, Mars.

universe: everything that exists everywhere.

weightless: the sensation of having no gravity pulling you down.

winter solstice: the shortest day of the year. December 21 in the Northern Hemisphere.

STELLAR WEB SITES

A Virtual Journey into the Universe
http://library.thinkquest.org/28327

Amazing Space
http://amazing-space.stsci.edu/

Artyastro
www.artyastro.com/main.htm

Cosmic Quest
www.childrensmuseum.org/cosmicquest

Discovery Education
http://school.discoveryeducation.com

Earth and Moon Viewer
http://formilab.ch/earthview/vplanet.html

Enchanted Learning: Zoom Astronomy
www.enchantedlearning.com

HubbleSite
http://hubblesite.org

Mars Exploration Rover Mission
http://marsrovers.jpl.nasa.gov/home

Mysteries of Deep Space
www.pbs.org/deepspace

NASA: Human Space Flight
http://spaceflight.nasa.gov/index.html

NASA Science Fun
http://science.hq.nasa.gov/kids

NASA Space Place
http://spaceplace.nasa.gov/en/kids

National Geographic
www.nationalgeographic.com/solarsystem

Science News for Kids
www.sciencenewsforkids.org

Solar System Exploration
http://solarsystem.nasa.gov

Space
www.space.com

Starchild
http://starchild.gsfc.nasa.gov

The Exploratorium: Observatory
www.exploratorium.edu/observatory

Views of the Solar System
www.solarviews.com

Windows to the Universe
www.windows.ucar.edu

DOCUMENTARIES

In The Shadow of The Moon. NASA, 2007

OUT OF THIS WORLD SCIENCE MUSEUMS & PLANETARIUMS

To find a science museum in your city, check out this link: **www.museumca.org/cgi-bin/ cgiwrap/museumca/usa_search.cgi**. Enter "science" into the query, then wait for your results. Maybe you'll be able to plan a trip to one of these places soon.

Adler Planetarium & Astronomy Museum, Chicago, IL www.adlerplanetarium.org

American Museum of Natural History, New York, NY www.amnh.org

California Science Center, Los Angeles, CA www.nyhallsci.org

Carnegie Science Center, Pittsburgh, PA http://www.carnegiesciencecenter.org/

Center of Science and Industry, Columbus, OH www.cosi.org

Cleveland Museum of Natural History, Cleveland, OH www.cmnh.org

Denver Museum of Nature and Science, Denver, CO www.dmns.org

Fernbank Science Center, Atlanta, GA http://fsc.fernbank.edu

The Franklin Institute Science Museum, Philadelphia, PA http://www2.fi.edu

Kopernik Observatory and Science Center, Vestal, NY www.kopernik.org

Griffith Observatory, Los Angeles, CA www.griffithobs.org

Hayden Planetarium Rose Center for Earth and Space, New York, NY http://haydenplanetarium.org

New York Hall of Science, Queens, NY www.nyhallsci.org/

Smithsonian National Air and Space Museum, Washington, DC www.nasm.si.edu

A

activities
  ancient solar observatory, 32
  asteroid tool belt, 58
  astronaut emergency game, 60
  Big Bang tag, 9
  constellation shadow puppets, 88
  edible phases of the moon, 43
  ellipse, 21
  gyroscope, 48
  magnetic orbiting earth, 23
  Mars rover, 72
  meteor crater pudding, 77
  meteor shower snowglobe, 80
  mini planetarium, 87
  origami solar system mobile, 12–13
  papier-mâché globe, 22
  race across the galaxy scavenger
    hunt, 10–11
  race to the moon board game, 46–47
  rings of Saturn whirligig, 70
  robotic arm, 57
  shooting comet wheel, 79
  solar eclipse, 34–35
  solar oven, 33
  space probe, 71
  space shuttle, 44–45
  travel with the stars game, 86
  wearable space suit, 59
Aldrin, Edwin "Buzz," 42, 53
Armstrong, Neil, 42, 53
asteroids, 73–75
astronauts, 11, 42, 49–56, 58–59,
  60. *See also* space travel
astronomical units, 8
atmosphere, 16–18, 31, 38, 63–64, 76
auroras, 30–31

B

Big Bang, 9
Big Dipper, 84

C

calendars, 26, 32, 41
Canis Major, 45
Cassiopeia, 68
Ceres, 67, 74–75
climate, 15–16, 18, 38. *See also*
  temperatures
comets, 73, 74, 75, 76–81
constellations, 6, 15, 35, 45, 54, 62,
  68, 75, 83–84, 88,
continents, 19–20
Copernicus, Nicolaus, 6
Cynus, 35

D

Draco, 75
dwarf planets, 5, 62, 65, 67, 75

E

Earth, 4, 7, 8, 14–20, 25, 31, 76, 83
eclipses, 27, 30, 34
energy, solar, 28–29, 33, 52

G

Gagarin, Yury, 11, 42
galaxy, 3, 85, 87
Galilei, Galileo, 17, 29, 62, 64, 66
gases, 18, 27–29, 31, 65–66, 83, 85
global warming, 18
Goddard, Robert, 37
gravity, 5, 6, 12, 18, 30, 37–38,
  50–51, 55–56, 70, 74
greenhouse gases, 18

H

Halley's comet (Edmund Halley), 77–78
Herschel, Caroline, 78
Herschel, William, 63, 78
Hubble, Edwin (Hubble Space
  Telescope), 87

I

International Space Station, 51–52

J

Jovian planets, 4, 65–67. *See also*
  Jupiter; Neptune; Saturn; Uranus
Jupiter, 4, 7, 62, 65–66

K

Kepler, Johannes, 23, 69

L

Lippershey, Hans, 20
Little Dipper, 6

M

Mars, 4, 7, 62–64, 72
Mercury, 4, 7, 62–63
meteors/meteorites, 38, 73, 75–76,
  80, 81
Milky Way galaxy, 3, 85
moon, 30, 36–43, 46, 53, 65–66

N

NASA, 42
nebula, 6, 83
Neptune, 4, 7, 62, 63, 65–67
Newton, Isaac, 30
North Star, 6

O

observatories, 9, 26, 32

orbit, 5, 12, 16, 23, 36, 50–52,
  62, 66–67, 69, 77–78, 79
Orion, 54, 88

P

Piazzi, Giuseppi, 75
planets, 3–7, 9, 12, 16, 23
  61–69, 75
Pluto, 4–5, 62, 65, 67
Polaris (North Star), 6
pollution, 18
Ptolemy, 5

S

Saturn, 4, 7, 62, 64, 65–66, 70
seasons, 16
Shepard, Alan, 41
Sirius (Dog Star), 45
solar energy, 28–29, 33, 52
solar flares, 29
solar system, 3–9. *See also* asteroids;
  comets; meteors; planets; sun
solar wind, 31
solstice, winter and summer, 26
Southern Cross, 15
space suits, 52–53, 59
space travel, 11, 19, 28, 37, 38,
  40, 41, 42, 44, 49–56, 58–59,
  62–64, 66–67, 68, 69, 71, 72,
  77. *See also* astronauts
stars, 6, 45, 82–86. *See also*
  constellations; sun
sun, 5–8, 12, 15–16, 25–34, 40, 83

T

telescopes, 17, 20, 29, 30, 62–63,
  78, 87
temperatures, 18, 27–28, 29, 38,
  64, 65
Tereshkova, Valentina, 68
terrestrial planets, 4, 63–64. *See*
  also Earth; Mars; Mercury; Venus

U

universe, 3, 87
Uranus, 4, 7, 62, 63, 65–67
Ursa Major, 84

V

Venus, 4, 7, 62–64, 66

W

water, 15, 39, 55
weather. *See* climate
weightlessness, 50–51, 55–56
White, Edward Higgins, 56